DERBYSHIRE PLACE-NAMES

ANTHONY POULTON-SMITH

First published in 2005 by
Sutton Publishing Limited · Phoenix Mill
Thrupp · Stroud · Gloucestershire · GL5 2BU

British Library Cataloguing in Publication Data
A catalogue record for this book is available from the British Library.

ISBN 0-7509-3925-7

Typeset in 11.5/14pt Garamond.
Typesetting and origination by
Sutton Publishing Limited.
Printed and bound in England by
J.H. Haynes & Co. Ltd, Sparkford.

FOREWORD

My interest in ley lines, the ancient pathways and tracks which linked the hillforts and earliest settlements of our islands, inevitably led to a similar fascination with place-names and their origins. Many of the markers for the leys, as clear as the largest motorway sign to the travellers of the day, are now lost and the only remaining evidence is in the name of the place.

Since 1974 the boundaries of a number of counties have been redrawn in order to satisfy the politics of the day. Derbyshire has suffered much less than most in this respect but in order to encompass those areas which have been involved in such changes, and for those who now find themselves outside the county of their birth, I have included as many places as possible which have at some time been part of the county. The basic alphabetical format of the following pages lists the main towns, villages and parishes, together with minor place-names, districts, roads, streets, fields and pub names for the area.

My sincere gratitude is due to all those who have assisted me in the preparation of this book. Particular mention should be made of the libraries at Matlock, Buxton and Swadlincote. A special thank you, too, to my mother Mrs Doreen Smith, without whom this book would not have been possible. I hope you find as much pleasure in reading this book as I had in writing it.

We are indebted to photographer Andy Savage whose website is a valuable source for any Derbyshire historian. It can be found at www.derbyphotos.co.uk

Derby riverside gardens at night. (Photo: Andy Savage)

INTRODUCTION

England's place-names are predominantly derived from Old English or Saxon, the language spoken by the occupants of Britain from the end of the Roman era. By the Middle Ages Middle England had evolved, from which the modern form of the language developed. Derbyshire's place-names also had another important influence as it lay on the edge of the Danelaw, where Danes and other Scandinavian peoples held sway before the Norman Conquest. All over this area place-names still indicate their Scandinavian origins.

Yet it should not be assumed that all place-names were created by these two cultures alone. Prior to the Roman era the region was inhabited by Celtic peoples, who spoke a language closely related to Gaelic, Welsh, Cornish and the Breton tongue still sometimes used in Brittany. The Celtic group also contributed to modern place-names, particularly in relation to topographical features such as mountains and rivers. That such ancient languages still exist is of great benefit when defining place-names, for no written records exist.

Many definitions of streams and rivers, hills and mountains may seem over-simplistic, with origins such as 'water, flowing, spring' or 'hill, summit, ridge'. Yet even today it is unusual to mention local features by name in the normal course of conversation – anglers for example might announce they are going to 'the river', or ramblers to walk 'the hills'.

While the Romans are justifiably renowned for their technological achievements, when it comes to place-names they were content simply to 'Latinise' existing names and contributed few if any new names, except by virtue of their occupation (as any schoolchild knows, names ending in -cester and -chester are indicative of a Roman fort, yet even this is derived from the Saxon word *caester*, and is not Latin). As with territories, technology, peoples and even gods, the Romans relentlessly assimilated each new conquest into their culture, and the same principle applied to place-names. The Roman Empire is synonymous with the building of an efficient and widespread network of roads. While this notable achievement should not be understated, in truth what they really did was build a durable and long-lasting surface along trackways that had already existed for thousands of years by the time Rome was founded in 753 BC.

When people abandoned the life of the hunter-gatherer and settled down to an agricultural existence, they built their shelters on the tops of hills. With a wooden palisade and/or ditch encircling the encampment, they were safer from potential enemy attack, could protect valuable livestock, and minimised the very real threat of flooding. Naturally these communities were largely self-sufficient, but there was always a shortage of something and a surfeit of another and they were able to trade their surplus for something they lacked. Salt, an important preserving agent for meat, was an important early commodity.

At this time the landscape of England was very different from today, as deciduous forests gave way to conifers on higher ground in a virtually unbroken woodland blanket pierced only by the occasional hilltop with its resident community. A man in a hillfort could see his neighbours – but once below the forest canopy he could easily lose his way. Hence men carrying staves would mark the route, nearly always in a straight line from start to destination, aligning the staves and leaving markers along the way. These markers or signposts could be anything that stood out as man-made in the landscape: a pile of stones, a tree deliberately burned, or stepping stones across a stream. Before long the marked pathways became distinct tracks, established by use. While the markers have long since disappeared, a few examples still survive today in place-names.

These trackways were arteries through what was virtually a wilderness, allowing the traveller a comparatively safe and direct journey. Many of these ancient tracks are found along paths known as ley lines, thought by some to mark lines of force which form part of the natural environment. Now whether the pathways follow these lines of force, or if the pathways merely invoked a feeling of well-being, is a matter of much scepticism and discussion and is not really relevant within the pages of this book. What is certain is that these ancient tracks did exist, they are invariably straight as the proverbial arrow, and sites of historical importance are found along them. Doubters point out that since there are so many churches, crossroads, tumuli, stone circles, fords, and so on, in the landscape, it is inevitable that many will appear to form straight lines; the reverse argument – that the existence of the paths gave rise to such 'markers' along them – has as many credible elements as implausible ones. For our purposes, the 'marker' names simply exist and their meaning is clear, which is all that need be considered here.

The method used to define a place-name depends on just what the 'place' is – it could be a town, village, field, river, mountain, Roman road, modern street or public house. However, all require us to find as many forms of the name, over as long a time period, as possible. Where topographical features are concerned, such as rivers and mountains, the earliest forms of the names are not normally recorded. Thus we must rely on comparisons with known languages, as discussed earlier. The names of public houses are also a special case and require separate discussion.

Derby Guildhall. (Photo: Andy Savage)

The splendid Baslow church has a clock on just two faces of the tower. One face displays the usual Roman numerals, while the second commemorates the Diamond Jubilee of Queen Victoria.

In tracking down the earlier names of our towns and villages there are a number of documents in existence which may assist in our endeavours but none of these can be accepted as entirely accurate, especially the best-known work of them all, Domesday. Many of the 'original' documents preserved today are actually very old copies, made because the earlier record was becoming tattered and illegible. Here we encounter three problems. First, only a very small proportion of the population could read or write, an obvious stumbling-block. Secondly, the scribes had their own notions as to grammar and spelling, and they had no dictionary or set rules to follow (Shakespeare himself is known to have used several spellings of his own name, and he lived centuries after the vast majority of today's place-names were already set in stone).

Thirdly, there is the obvious risk of errors creeping in as hand-written copies were made from an already damaged original, a problem compounded as successive copies were produced. Even a single letter misread from the original form could change the intended meaning, particularly when it comes to proper names. Domesday had an additional obstacle as three quite different languages were involved: the Old English of the illiterate Saxon (Scandinavian or Danish) inhabitants, who provided the basic information; the Old French of those conducting the census; and the form of stylised Latin used by the scribes compiling the finished work.

Thus we need to gather as many forms of the name as possible if we are to have any chance of defining its origin. Furthermore, we need to know where and when these early records were produced, which in turn gives us a clue as to the language(s) spoken by those involved.

Definitions of road- and street-names are researched in much the same way, except that they are invariably from more recent times. This is advantageous as the language is less of a barrier and the records available for consultation are greater in number and more accurate.

When it comes to defining the origins of pub names, it is important to understand just how our inns, taverns and hotels have evolved. Many have unusual names that are only to be found on the swinging signs outside our local. The very earliest names which can be attributed to a known origin date from the Roman era. During the Roman occupation of Britain, when few people could read or write, traders used symbols to inform their potential customers of what was on offer within. Many barbers still display the barber's pole, instantly recognisable even in modern times. In Roman Britain, innkeepers used a wreath of vine leaves for the same purpose, it being a representation of Bacchus, the god of wine.

A millennium later, when travelling on horseback became more commonplace, refreshment stops were required and enterprising individuals were quick to take advantage of this new market. Their customers were still largely illiterate, and so the ale stake was born. The 'stake' might be a prominent tree, or a long stout pole erected specifically for the purpose (very reminiscent of the pub sign supports of today). On the ale stake was tied a sheaf of barley, representing the major ingredient in brewing.

As time passed the ale-house replaced these home breweries, retaining the ale stake but becoming more adventurous with what was displayed. Already many establishments were known as much by the ale stake tree as by the barley tethered there, and thus it was almost inevitable that an image of the tree would replace the barley. Soon after, landowners or sponsors were acknowledged with some heraldic image, which explains why pub names feature so many oddly coloured animals – indeed Red Lion is by far the most popular pub name in the land.

By the latter half of the twentieth century sign painters were constantly looking for original ways to depict 'traditional' pub names, while breweries began to move away from traditional names in favour of more inventive (often humorous) though traditional-sounding names.

When the origins of a place-name are uncertain, there is a tendency to create fanciful derivations when the true origin is almost certainly ridiculously simple. In centuries to come historians will doubtless offer several complex and contrived explanations for modern pub names such as the Pig & Whistle; perhaps we should record here and now that that particular example was created as a pub name and has no fanciful etymology whatsoever.

The pub sign for The Gate Inn at Loscoe.

Common Place-
Name Elements

Element	Origin	Meaning
banke	OScand	bank, hill-slope
beau	OFrench	fine, beautiful
bekkr	OScand	stream
berg	OScand	hill
both	OScand	temporary shelter
broc	OE	brook, stream
burh	OE	fortified place
burna	OE	stream
by	OScand	farmstead, village
caester	OE	Roman stronghold
cirice	OE	church
clif	OE	cliff, slope, or bank
cnoll	OE	hill-top
cot	OE	cottage
cumb	OE	valley (particularly a short valley)
dael	OE	valley
dalr	OScand	valley
denu	OE	valley
dic	OE	ditch
dun	OE	hill
eg	OE	island, dry ground in marshland
feld	OE	tract of land cleared of trees
fenn	OE	marsh
ford	OE	river-crossing
gata	OScand	gate
geat	OE	gap, pass

Element	Origin	Meaning
halh	OE	corner of land
ham	OE	homestead
hamm	OE	water meadow
holmr	OScand	island, dry ground in marsh
holt	OE	wood, thicket
hyll	OE	hill
hyrst	OE	wooded hill
kjarr	OScand	church
leah	OE	woodland glade
port	OE	market-place
stan	OE	stone
stoc	OE	secondary or special place
stow	OE	assembly place
thorp	OScand	secondary or outlying farmstead
throp	OE	hamlet
thveit	OScand	clearing
tun	OE	farmstead, village
wella	OE	spring, stream
wic	OE	specialised farm (especially dairy)
worthig	OE	enclosed settlement

A

Abney

A Saxon or Old English name which is recorded as *Habenai* in Domesday, becoming *Abbeneia* at the end of the twelfth century. This is 'Abba's island'; the original second element here is *eg* which, although generally referring to an island, can also be used to describe any dry ground in a predominantly wet area. Furthermore the lower-lying wetland could often be seasonal, as was probably the case with Abney. The place-name is duplicated locally in **Abney Clough**, **Abney Grange**, **Abney Low** and **Abney Moor**, all having obvious additions.

Local field-names of interest include **Birchway Hat**, which is a 'birch-covered hat-shaped hill', and **Pudding Hole** a common minor name which always refers to muddy or sticky land.

Alderwasley

Recorded as *Alrewaseleg* in 1251 and as *Alrewasseleye* just thirty years later, there are three Saxon elements to this name: *alor-waesse-leah*. The first element is as it appears in the modern form, a *waesse* is alluvial land (liable to flooding), and the common place-name suffix *leah* refers to a woodland clearing. Putting all these together we can define Alderwasley as 'swamp in the clearing of alder trees', the name also being adopted for the local minor names of **Alderwasley Hall**, **Alderwasley Mill** and **Alderwasley Park**. The origins of the name may not be in doubt, yet the pronunciation of Alderwasley has been a touchy subject for many years. It was once regarded as a sign of social incompetence if one attempted to pronounce all four syllables, 'Arrowsly' and 'Allersly' being acceptable.

While the modern form is somewhat corrupted, early records show there is no doubt that **Wiggonlee Farm** comes from 'Wicga's woodland clearing'. **Milnhay** is much closer to the original 'mill enclosure'.

Aldwark

From the Saxon *eald-weorc*, listed as *Aldwerke* in 1140, this name indicates an 'old fortification'. This is a good example of how defining a name can reveal something more about a place. Although the only historical record we have dates from the middle of the twelfth century, the fact that the name is clearly

Saxon in origin tells us that a settlement must have existed here before the Norman Conquest. In addition, the use of the 'old' element tells us that it must have been the site of a fortified settlement many years before this, possibly pre-dating the Roman occupation. By contrast the comparatively recent **Aldwark Grange** has the same origins.

Alfreton

A record of 1002 speaks of *Aelfredington*, Domesday speaks of *Elstretune*, while the modern form appears surprisingly early in 1236. Domesday's entries are invariably erroneous, so normally we would take the earlier version which would give 'the settlement of the followers or people of Aelfred'. However, this personal name was not common until the late Saxon era, which would suggest the actual personal name here was Aelfhere. Local names of the same origin include **Alfreton Common**, **Alfreton Hall**, **Alfreton Park** and **Alfreton Brook**, the latter taking its name from the place, a process known as back-formation. It seems likely that Alfreton Brook had an earlier name but this is now lost.

While darts and dominoes are considered the traditional pub games, **The Double Six** is a modern reminder that ever since Roman times various indoor games have been a vital ingredient in the social life of an inn. **The Corner Pin**

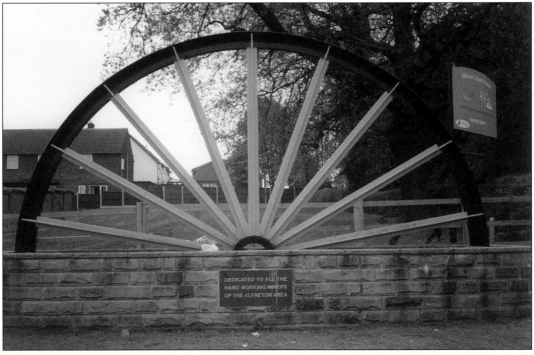

Alfreton miners' monument, featuring part of the winding gear from a mine, in honour of all those in the area who worked in the mining industries.

is derived from the game of skittles, the pin in question being on the outside and thus the most difficult to knock down.

Greenhill Lane is named after the family from Greenhill in Norton who held land here from the thirteenth century, while the **Riddings** is a fairly common minor place-name simply meaning 'the clearings'. **Swanwick Delves** has nothing to do with water-fowl but is 'the dairy farm of the herdsmen'. **Copthorne Villas** stood near 'a pollarded thorn tree'. **Fletcher's Yard** was held by John Fletcher in 1741, while **Hockley** is of Old English origins as '(place at) Hocca's clearing'.

Alkmonton

As with Alfreton, the few early forms of this name do not clarify the personal name. Domesday's *Alchementune* and *Alcmunton* in 1242 point to this place once being 'the village of Ealhmund or Alhmund'. One minor place-name in Alkmonton is not unusual in its origins – indeed almost half of all parishes in England have at least one similar name – but **Seven Days Math** does have a very unusual final element. This, as with other field-names including a number, refers to the length of time required to plough the land.

Allestree

It is very unusual for a place-name to have such a suffix, and the normal modern form would be -try. Derived from the Old English *treow*, it means exactly what it seems, this being 'Aethelheard's tree'. The tree in question would have been notable as a boundary marker or as a meeting-place (possibly for a religious rite). **Allestree Hall** and **Allestree Park** share this origin.

Alport

The only surviving record of note is that of *Aldeport* from 1276. While a 'port' so far inland may seem strange, the Saxon *port* meant simply a 'town' – in this case 'the old town'. It is also found locally as **Alport Castle, Alport Farm, Alport Grain, Alport Head, Alport Moor** and the **Alport River**; the latter's original name is now lost.

Alsop en la Dale

Elleshope in 1086, *Aleshop* in 1241 and *Alsope in le dale* in 1535 are the only records of note. Here the Old English *hop* is preceded by a personal name giving 'valley of a man named Aelle'. The later suffix of the sixteenth century is a Norman-French addition meaning 'in the valley': clearly the original meaning of the name was unknown by then.

Alton

The only surviving record dates from 1296 in the modern form. Derived from the Old English elements *ald-tun*, this is 'the old settlement'. Certainly this was not the original name of the settlement, but sadly nothing survives to offer even the smallest clue as to what this place was once called.

Alvaston

Alvaston Church contains a Saxon coffin lid, indicating that Saxons lived in the village. This gives a clue to the origin here. This is probably 'Aethelwald's farmstead', although the personal name could be Aelfwald. Unfortunately the two surviving records of *Alewaldestune* in 1002 and *Aelwoldestun* in Domesday do not offer conclusive proof.

Boulton is a local name derived from 'Bola's farmstead'; **Allenton** recalls a Mr Allen who organised the building of houses here in the late nineteenth century; **Osborne Cottage** was home to William Osborn in 1622; **Stanhope Villa** recalls former resident Lady Anne Stanhop in 1555; and **Crewton** (previously known as **Newton**) was renamed in honour of the building programme started by Sir Vauncey Crewe.

A local pub, the **Blue Peter**, is not named after the children's television series which is now entertaining the grandchildren of its early viewers, but is taken from the flag flown by a ship about to leave port – probably the symbol of a landlord or landowner with maritime connections.

Amber, River

Many river-names (and hill-names too) originate from the British or Celtic tongue which is related to modern Welsh, Cornish and Breton and was the predominant language in Derbyshire prior to the arrival of the Romans, and indeed right through Roman times up to the arrival of the Saxons in the fifth and sixth centuries. Except for the more common elements, place-names derived from the British tongues are often unclear, largely because the available records date from a much later era and the names have become corrupted to an unintelligible degree.

The Amber is one such example (only *Ambre* from 1191 survives), although it is possible to offer an explanation. Even today we commonly refer to the local river simply as simply 'the river', without using its real name. Doubtless the inhabitants of these islands did the same two thousand years ago. So despite the original word being unknown in the case of the Amber, we do know that similar words existed in two of the languages from the Indo-European group which were widely used in the same era. Sanskrit *ambhas*, meaning 'water', and Latin *imber,* 'shower', can easily be seen to be related to the (unknown) origin of Amber. Thus whatever the exact meaning, we can be fairly certain that Amber was simply a reference to water.

Apperknowle

Pronunciation has affected the spelling of the name somewhat, but the Old English *apuldor-cnoll* is clearly the origin – as seen in the records of *Apelknol* in 1317 and *Apuurknoll* in 1467. There can be no doubt this place was once known as 'apple-tree hill'.

Arleston

For once the Domesday version of *Erlestune* is not unlike that *Erleston* recorded at the end of the thirteenth century. These earlier forms differ little from the original sense of 'the earl's tun or settlement'.

Ash

While it may seem pointless to mention the early forms of *Aesce* in 987, *Eisse* in 1086 and *Eyss* in 1242 simply to show this was the '(place at) the ash-trees', there are many examples of names of seemingly obvious origin being corrupted over the intervening centuries. Such corruptions can often change not only the sense but the entire meaning.

Ashbourne

Found as *Esseburne* in Domesday, *Esseburn* in 1188, and *Ascheburn* in the early thirteenth century, this is predictably 'the stream where ash-trees grow'. This is the early name of what is today known as **Henmoor Brook**, a name of uncertain origin, the first element invariably a corrupted personal name. **Ashbourne Hall** has identical origins. The present church at Ashbourne dates from the reign of Henry III (1216–72), although there was certainly an earlier building pre-dating the Norman Conquest.

Ashbourne's local names of now and yesteryear include **St Johns Street**, which marks the location of the Knights Hospitaller of St John; **Back Bridge**, a corrupted form of the original 'Betta's bridge'; and **Harvey Cottage**, the home of Thomas Hervi as early as 1260. However, it is **Dig Street** which has the most intriguing history. It is recorded first in 1276 as *unam altam viam apud Lovedich,* and as Loveditche in 1380, while the first modern version appears in 1630 as *Digstreet.* We can only assume this was Ashbourne's Lovers Lane, with the centuries eroding the first element from 'ditch' to 'dig'.

The unusual sign for the Green Man & Black's Head Royal Hotel in Ashbourne (see previous page).

Ashford

The '(place at) the ford where ash-trees grow', as evidenced by the listings as *Aescforda* in 926 and *Aisseford* in Domesday. Among the more interesting field-names locally we find **Piga-seats** where the first element is derived from the personal name Pigot and the suffix is Saxon *sceat* meaning 'nook, corner of land'. There is also **Magpie Mine**, which takes its name from a boundary stone named after a lady named Margaret, as was a nearby hill. Sadly nothing more is known of this person.

Ashleyhay

This name has changed little since appearing as *Asslewehay* in 1255 and *Asshelehay* in 1309. Derived from the Saxon *aescleah*, this is 'the enclosure among the ash-trees'.

Locally **Alport Hill**, 'the hill by the old town', takes its name from the place-name. In the river-name **Colebrook** we find a common corruption where Cole-, or more often Coal-, has replaced the original 'cold brook'. **Spout** comes from the Old English word *spoute*, 'spring of water'. The field-name **Dead Carr** derives from the Old Norse *dead-kjarr* suggesting 'an infertile marsh'. Lastly **Spendlove Farm** recalls the residency of John Spendlove in 1829.

Ashop

From the original Old English *aesc-hop*, through *Essop* and *Asshope* in the early thirteenth century, the name has changed little from its origins as 'valley of the ash-trees'. Local place-names share the same element, including **Ashop Clough**, **Ashop Farm**, **Ashop Head**, **Ashop Moor**, **Nether Ashop** and **Ashop River**. It is possible that the place took its name from the river or vice versa;, either would fit the origins.

Ashover

Clearly Derbyshire had great numbers of ash-trees considering the number of place-names with the Saxon element *aesc*. The second element here is also Old English, referring to a ridge of land. Early listings include Domesday's *Essovre* and *Esshovere* from 1252.

Ashover's parish church provides much information on residents of the past. David Wall's memorial mentions his superior bassoon playing, while a list of incumbents shows the church had only eight rectors between 1621 and 1942. Joseph Nodder took the position during the reign of William IV (1830-7), eventually handing over to his son John Nodder who worked until he was unable to continue, finally relinquishing the post during the reign of George VI (1936-52). Between them they had seen six monarchs on the throne: William IV, Queen Victoria, Edward VII, George V, Edward VIII and George VI.

Minor place-names in and near Ashover include **Buntingfield**, which recalls the Bunting family, prominent here from the fourteenth century; Butterley, 'the clearing with good pasture' (producing good butter); **Clattercotes Farm**, 'the cottages near a pile of stones'; and the somewhat obscure **Press** which is uncertain but may be related to the early Welsh word *pres* meaning 'brushwood'. **Cullumbell House** was the home of John Columbell in 1409; his family were particularly prominent in neighbouring Darley. Leonard Wheatcroft's biographer relates how he built the **House of Fabrick** on the hill in 1691, but does not give any clues as to why he named it such or whether the name existed prior to this date. **Rattle** takes its name from the Rattel family who were here by 1694, while **Spitewinter** is an uncomplimentary comment on the suitability of this particular plot of land.

Aston (near Hope)

Domesday's *Estune* shows this common place-name is 'the eastern tun (settlement)'. Furthermore the name also tells us a little about the history of the place, for it shows that it grew as an outlying post to the east of the original settlement, which was probably an agricultural centre.

Aston-upon-Trent

Another 'eastern tun', the suffix clearly referring to its situation alongside the river. The name was also applied locally to **Aston Hall**, **Aston Moor**, **Astonhill** and **Astonhill Farm**. The village has an impressive church of Norman design, and the tower and a few windows still survive from this period.

Atlow

Recorded as *Etelawe* in 1086 and *Atteloue* in 1215, this name is derived from 'Eatta's burial-mound'. Later there appears a secondary name within the parish of **Atlow Winn**, the addition from Old English *wynne* indicating a 'pasture'.

Ault Hucknall

Listed as *Hokenhale* in 1291 and *Hukenalle* in 1428, this place-name is derived from Old English 'Hucca's *halh*', used here in the sense of 'valley'. The additional Ault is thought to be derived from Old French *haut*, meaning 'high'.

Minor place-names here show that residents in the pre-Conquest era were both Scandinavian and Saxon, or at least had personal names suggesting such origins. **Batley Farm** is located at 'Bata's woodland clearing, **Blingsby Gate** was once the entrance to 'Blaeingr's farm'; and **Hardstoft** was 'Hert's homestead'. **Astwith** is an early indicator of the growth of the community for it tells of the '(place at) the east woodland clearing'.

The church at Ault Hucknall, dedicated to St John the Baptist. The church holds the remains of the philosopher Thomas Hobbes.

B

Bakewell

Although Bakewell has not grown to anywhere near the size of other well-known towns and cities, its name is familiar across most of the English-speaking world and beyond, courtesy of the entry under 'Tarts' in most cookery books, although it should correctly be referred to as a pudding. Bakewell was also recognised by Josiah Wedgwood for its abundant supply of the hard flint-like rock chert, used extensively in the making of pottery.

It is found as early as AD 924 as *Badecan wiellon* and as *Badecanwelle* twenty-five years later, while Domesday's version is *Bodeqvella*, and an entry from the mid-thirteenth century speaks of *Bauquell*. Despite the later corruptions, the early forms clearly show this to be '(the place at) Badeca's spring or stream'. Nothing is known of this person. Locally we also find the five-arched **Bakewell Bridge** built about 1300, which has identical origins, while **The Yeld** and **Yeld Road** are derived from the Saxon *helde* meaning 'slope'.

Local names of interest include **Wigger Dale**, the early forms of which are too erratic to say for certain if this is 'Wycga's stream' from Old English *wigga* meaning 'beetle', or even from an earlier use of *wigga* as 'one that moves'. **Outrake** tells us this was 'the way to the outer fields or open land' (and presumably the way back again too); **Ballcross** comes from Saxon *ball-cros* '(place at) the cross on the hill'; and **Higgenholes** speaks of 'Hickin's hollows', where the personal name is derived from Hick, itself a diminutive form of Richard. **The Manners** remembers a prominent family of Whig supporters who owned a number of public houses. They were probably better known as the Earls of Pembroke. This name is interesting for most of their premises simply had the word 'Blue' added to the existing name to show their political allegiance. The earliest inn 'signs' were merely pointers to show that ale was brewed within. Few markers were simpler than the sheaf of barley, which was soon copied as the **Wheatsheaf**.

Ballidon

Listings from the latter half of the eleventh century as *Belidene* and *Balidene* show this to be derived from Old English *baelgdenu*, which describes the 'sack-like valley'. The first element here is *belg* or *boelg*, literally meaning 'bag'. The name is also represented in **Ballidonhall Farm** and **Ballidonmoor**. Less certain is **Royston Grange**, which could be either 'reeve's stones' or 'raven's stones', which was the property of Garendon Abbey in Leicestershire.

Bamford

Domesday's *Banford* is the earliest known record, while by 1228 the name is found in the modern form. Bamford's origins give us a glimpse of the area in those times, for this was the '(place at) the ford with a beam', the beam telling us this was a fairly unusual ford in also having a footbridge. Furthermore, we can also deduce there must have been a need for a footbridge, probably because (at least at certain times of the year) the river was too deep or swift to ford safely.

Bamford Clough and **Bamford Edge** are among the minor place-names here. This is the region known as **Mytham Bridge**, the modern bridge itself standing just below where the Noe and Overdale join the Derwent. The name reflects this as the '(place at) the meeting of the streams'. **The Tucker** recalls the Tucker family who were here in 1786, while **Sickleholme Golf Course** stands on the 'small stream in the water meadow', from Old Norse *sicel holmr*.

Barlborough

Here we have a place-name which has never conclusively been defined. It is listed as *Barleburh* in 1002 and *Barleburg* in Domesday, and these records would normally suggest a personal name followed by the Saxon *burg*, 'a fortified place'. However, we know of no suitable personal name. There is a possibility that the first element here is Saxon *barleah*, 'boar woodland clearing', and indeed this may well have been the original name for the place.

The **Rose & Crown** is one of the most common pub names in the country. It first appeared in the early seventeenth century as an indication of the proprietors' loyalty to the crown. Many pubs across the length and breadth of England take the name **Apollo Inn** from the Greek god. The Greeks also considered Apollo to be the bringer and curer of plagues, which led to his figure being included by the apothecaries in their coat of arms. This is the major reason for the number of pubs named after the Greek god today, although the signs for these establishments invariably portray him in classic pose.

Barlow

Early records as *Barleie* in 1066, *Barlee* in 1203, *Barleia* in 1207, and *Barlegh* in 1230 point to the same origins as Barlborough, from Old English *bar-leah*, 'woodland clearing where boars are seen'. However, it is possible the origin here may be *baer-leah*, in which case the first element would refer to the growing of barley here. **Barlow Common**, **Barlow Grange**, **Barlow Lees**, **Barlow Moor**,

Barlow Woodseats and **Barlow Brook** all take their names from the place, the river-name providing another example of back-formation.

Other local names of note include **Sweetingsick Wood**, once known as 'the sweet apple spring'; **Black Car Lumb**, from the Old Norse *blaec kjarr lumm*, 'black pool overgrown with brushwood'; and **Wilkinhill** where the first element is a diminutive form of William, thus 'William's hill'.

The name of the **Hare & Hounds Inn** is more likely to be derived from a landlord who had some connection with the hunt, rather than a meeting-place for the hounds. From 'Cobnar's bank or slope' comes **Cobnar Wood**, the suffix 'wood' being a comparatively recent addition. **Oxten Rakes** refers to 'paths used by the ox or oxen'; **Highlightley Farm** is situated at 'the bright woodland clearing', a reference to the colour of the soil; and **Rumbling Street** is a reference to traffic noise, amazingly recorded as such as early as 1630!

Barrow upon Trent

The suffix, while self-explanatory, is necessary as Barrow is a very common place-name, which leads us to expect quite a simple meaning. Records such as *Bareuue* in Domesday and *Barewe* at the end of the twelfth century show this to be a 'grove' or 'wood' from Old English *bearu*. Locally **Barrow Old Elm** was named from a well-known landmark.

Barton Blount

Another common place-name is Barton. From the Saxon *beretun* meaning 'barley (or perhaps simply corn) settlement', it is found as *Barctune* in 1066, *Bartona* in 1165 and for the first time with its unique suffix in 1535 as *Bartonblonte*. As with many double-barrelled names, the addition is taken from the surname of former local landholders. Barton Blount is recorded as being held by Thomas Blount in 1428. Interestingly the place is recorded as Barton Bakepuys in that same year, while back in 1160 the landholder here was one R. de Bakepuz. Locally **Bartonfields** and **Bartonpark** took the main name, while the unusually named **Gostyfields** is the Saxon *gorstig-feld*, 'open country overgrown with gorse'.

Baslow

Recorded as *Basselau* in 1066, *Bassalawa* in 1157, *Bassela* in 1179 and *Basselowe* in 1242, this name is derived from 'Bassa's hill or burial mound'. **Mellor Lane** is named after Henry Mellar, a local dignitary who lived here around the end of the sixteenth century.

The splendid church here has a clock on two faces of the tower. One displays the usual Roman numerals, while the second (known as the Jubilee Clock) commemorates the Diamond Jubilee of Queen Victoria. It has no numbers but reads 'V I C T O R I A 1 8 9 7' instead.

Beard

Found as *Berde* in 1253 and *Berd* fifty years later, this is derived from Old English *brerd* meaning 'brim, bank'. Loss of the first 'r' over the centuries owing to lazy pronunciation would be expected. Beard Hall does stand on the side of a hill.

Bearwardcote

Records of *Beruedescote* and *Bereuuardescote* in 1066 and *Berwardecote* in 1281 might suggest this is 'the cottage of the bearward', although bearward is first seen in 1399. It is more likely that the first element here is the personal name Beornweard, who William of Malmesbury tells us was Abbot of Glastonbury.

The Rutland Arms at Baslow, depicting the arms of the dukes of Rutland and their motto, pour-y-parvenir, literally 'to reach there' and taken as 'achievement'.

Beauchief Abbey

Appearing as *Beuchef, Beauchef* and *Bellam Caput* in the thirteenth century, this is the '(place at) the beautiful headland', the name referring to a hill spur.

Beeley

Recorded as *Begelie* in Domesday, *Beegeleg* in 1205 and *Begalaia* at the end of the thirteenth century, there is no doubt this is 'Beage's woodland clearing'. Here we find minor place-names which mirror the main name, including the back-formation of **Beeley Brook**, together with **Beeley Hilltop**, **Beeley Moor** and **Beeley Plantation**. Also found locally is **Harland Edge** which was once thought to be named to reflect the hare population. Further investigation rejected the lagomorph origin in favour of 'boundary grove', indicating its position on the parish boundary. **Arkwright Plantation** was awarded to Richard Arkwright in 1832.

Beighton

Today's form is significantly different, disguising the true origins, and thus we need to consult the earlier forms of *Bectun* in 1002, *Bectune* in 1086, and *Becton* in 1236, which clearly show this to be 'the settlement by the brook'. Minor local names found in and around Beighton include **Hackenthorpe**, 'Haccin's outlying farmstead'; **Frecheville**, the family name of the lords of the manor of Staveley; **Nab Lane**, from Old Norse *nabbi-lanu* giving 'lane to the projecting peak or knoll'; and **Sothall**, 'Swotha's nook of land'.

Belper

Anyone who has been to the region will understand why this was known as *Beurepeir* and *Beurepeyr* in the mid-thirteenth century, for the name means 'beautiful retreat'. The name transfers to **Belper Bridge**, **Belper Lane** and **Belperland End**.

Lawn Cottage is a somewhat shortened modern version of the early records which tell of 'the glade belonging to Bradley', where Bradley is a place-name. We also find 'Wilheard's woodland clearing' today as **Wildersley Farm**, and 'Wigbald's copse' is now known as **Wyver Farm**.

The **Black Swan** at Belper, and elsewhere, is always derived from heraldic sources, usually of a prominent local family. However, until the discovery of Australia the black swan was considered to be a mythical creature, for all known swans were white. **Lord Nelson**, his ship and his battles have provided popular pub names since the early nineteenth century, while the **Welcome Tavern** is an obvious and fairly unusual invitation.

Belper, which is twinned with Pawtucket in Rhode Island, USA, was home to a cottage industry which began in the late eighteenth century when whole families were engaged in making nails. Today this is remembered by the local football team, nicknamed the Nailers.

Belph

The place takes its name from the stream. Listed as *Bolh*, *Belgh*, and *Belhismere* in the early fourteenth century, it comes from the Saxon name *Belge*, giving 'roaring river', which is related to both the Old English word *bylgian* and the Middle English *belwe*, 'to bellow, roar', and obviously describes the nature of the stream.

Birchill

Despite Domesday's somewhat misleading *Berceles*, there can be no doubt that the modern form means exactly what it seems as 'birch-covered hills'. This is confirmed by the record from 1347 as *Birchulles*.

Birchover

As with Birchill the birch tree is responsible for this name. Here we find records of *Barcouere*, *Birchoure* and the modern spelling as early as 1265, which all speak of a 'ridge overgrown with birch trees'. The name also appears in the locality as **Birchover Edge**.

Locally **Rowtor Rocks** is a large pile of gritstone rock standing some 18 metres above the surroundings. Rowtor means 'rough rock', a description which is certainly merited, while the second, seemingly superfluous, element is a relatively modern addition. **Sabinhay Farm** and **Wood** are derived from 'Sabin's enclosure' and hail from Norman times, as indicated by the personal name.

Often bearing on the sign a member of the pre-Christian religion, the **Druid Inn** actually refers to the Ancient Order of Druids, a friendly society founded in 1781 who held their meetings here.

Birley

There are no fewer than three places in Derbyshire with this name, near Beighton, Brampton and Hathersage. The name is derived from one of two Old English origins, either *byr-leah*, 'woodland clearing near a byre or cowshed', or *byrh-leah*, 'woodland clearing near a burg or fortified place'. None of the early records so far uncovered gives any indication as to which may be the more likely in any of the three places.

Blackwell

There are two Blackwells in Derbyshire. The one near Bakewell is recorded in Domesday as *Blacheuuelle*, while the place near Alfreton is given as *Blacwelle* in the same work. Despite the great differences they are undoubtedly derived from the '(place at) the black stream'.

Near Alfreton we find **Chee Dale** and **Chee Tor**, which early records show to be 'Ceof's valley', the same as **Chovesdale** of which it is a contraction. **Scanderlands** is a minor corruption of 'Sander's land', as it was in 1829, while **St Peter's Pike** tells of 'the stone point of St Peter'.

Bolsover

Despite the many records found, including *Belesovre* in 1086, *Bolesoura* in 1167, *Bulesoures* in 1197, and *Bolesor* in 1230, the origins of this name remain obscure. Certainly the second element is Saxon *ofer*, 'slope, edge of land', but the first remains a mystery. Some have suggested *bulan-loes*, 'bullock pasture', as the origin, but this has been discounted as the second element cannot be anything other than *ofer*, which does not fit with *bulan*. The same element is found in local names such as **Bolsover Castle**, **Bolsover Hill**, **Bolsover Moor** and **Bolsover Woodhouse**.

Bolsover Castle, an Elizabethan residence, was built on the site of an old Norman castle as an impressive reminder of the earlier age of chivalry and, despite its appearance, has no defensive features of note.

Other local names of note include **Brockley Wood**, 'the woodland clearing by a brook'; **Oxcroft**, the '(place at) the small enclosure for oxen'; **Shuttlewood**, from the Old English *scyt(t)els-wudu*, literally 'shuttle bar wood', probably referring to where shuttles for looms were cut; and **Carrvale**, of Old Norse origin in 'brushwood close'. **Bentinck Villas** took the family name of the Dukes of Portland, lords of the manor of Bolsover while **Stanfree** was 'the place free of stones'.

Bolsover's street-names, both past and present, leave little to the imagination with examples such as Market Place, Middle Street, Nether Street and Upper Street. It is a pity that the latter no longer exists for it would have been fun to see if we could have successfully campaigned to have its old name reinstated; it appears on a record dated 1623 as *le Superiore vico de Bols* – what an impression that would make on one's headed notepaper.

The **Black Bull** is instantly recognisable for it can only be a pub name. As with all pubs featuring a colour and an animal, it is taken from the coat of arms of either a family or a trade. Invariably these heraldic names defy all attempts to trace their origins, as is the case here.

Bonsall

Found as *Bunteshale* in Domesday, and *Bontishale* and *Bontesale* in the late thirteenth century, this is 'Bunt's corner of land'. The personal name itself is not recorded, but is thought to be a shortened form of Buntel, which is known. The name is also seen here in **Bonsall Dale**, **Bonsall Mill** and **Bonsall Moor**.

Slaley is derived from 'the clearing where sloes grow'; **Pounder Lane** is recorded as the home of William Poundall in 1783; while William Ruggs was at **Rugs Hall** in 1778. We also find the delightful name **Via Gellia**, which is named after the Gell family of Hopton, while the unofficial name coined by locals for a track where an old gate stood is **Clatterway**, which describes 'the loose stones track' perfectly. Another place-name created specifically to be noticed is **Beans and Bacon Mine**, a fanciful name of comparatively recent beginnings chosen for no (known) specific reason. If the reason is, as we suspect, simply to gain attention, then they are still succeeding in the twenty-first century, as this page proves.

Borrowash

This unusual place-name is found as *Burysasch* in 1272 and *Burwishasshe* just three years later. Clearly this is the '(place at) the ash by the burgh or fortified place'. However, there is reason to believe that the place was once known as just Burgh, indeed a record dating from 1269 speaks of a Burgh upon Derwent (although there is some disagreement as to whether this was actually the same place).

The tale of Noah's Ark, the ultimate 'disaster' in the Bible, is made welcoming by the sign featuring a rainbow – God's indication that never again would he wash the sinners from the face of the earth.

As with pub names featuring Druids, Masons and the like, **The Foresters** may today have a sign depicting a woodsman but the name's true origins derive from a friendly society which held its meetings here. The Ancient Order of Foresters has numerous lodges in Britain and the US (where they are known as 'courts').

The tale of Noah's Ark in the Bible is but one version of many 'flood' narratives found in just about every ancient culture. It is found as a pub name from the Middle Ages, when *The Deluge* was a popular mystery play. The ark also features in the arms of the Shipwrights' Company, perhaps indicating a link with an early landlord or owner.

Bottle Brook

This small tributary of the Derwent does not appear in surviving records before the sixteenth century so its interesting and rather unusual name is difficult to define with any certainty. However, it may be possible to establish the meaning by association, for close by are **Denby Bottles** and **Bottlebrook Houses**. Once again no early forms of these other names have been found, but it is likely that these (and thus the river-name) come from the Old English *bool-broc*, 'brook by a building'. Certainly such a building would have been either highly distinctive or of great significance. Unfortunately there is nothing to suggest any such building ever existed here.

Boulton

Listed as *Boletune* in Domesday, *Boletun* in 1176 and *Bolton* in 1250, there can be no doubt this was 'Bola's tun or settlement'.

Bowden Edge

Listed as *Boudone* in 1275 and *Boudon* in 1339, this name comes from the Old English *bog-dun* or *boge-dun*, 'arched or rounded hill'. The first element is derived from the Old English *boga*, 'bow'. The suffix is a fairly recent addition.

Boylestone

This appears as *Boilestun* in Domesday and as *Boilestunia*, *Bodeleston* and *Boylesto*n during the thirteenth century, and the final element appears to be the common Saxon *tun*, 'settlement', in which case we would expect it to follow a personal name. However, no known personal name can be attributed to the early forms quoted, which may mean the name derives instead from the Old English *bog-hyll* (as seen in **Boulton**), referring to the arched shape of the ridge on which the place stands. There is also a **Boylestonfield** locally, as well as **Awdishaw Lane**, which began life as 'the house where the alder trees grow'.

Boythorpe

Domesday's *Buitorp* and *Boythorp* some 150 years later are by no means conclusive, yet this is probably 'Boia's thorp (farm)'.

Brackenfield

From the Old Scandinavian *brakni-thveit*, listed as *Brachentheyt* in 1269 and *Brakinweyt* just three years later, Brackenfield began originally as the '(place at) the woodland clearing where bracken grows'. This seeming wilderness grew steadily over the centuries. **Ogston Hall** was built there and took its name from the land occupied by 'Oggod's farmstead'; **Skeggerleg** is a modern name which still sounds very medieval, being derived from 'leg-shaped wood'; **Shipman's Cottage** was the residence of Helen Shipman in 1751; and **Mather's Grave** recalls the last resting-place of Samuel Mather who committed the unforgivable sin of suicide in 1716.

Bradbourne

Even today it is easy to see the Saxon 'broad stream', which also appears here as **Bradbourne Hall** and **Bradbourne Mill**.

Bradley

This place-name is found throughout the Midlands, always with the same meaning of the '(place at) the broad woodland clearing', irrespective of the many varied spellings in ancient records (here seen as *Braidelei, Bradleye,* and *Bradele*). The original name of the watercourse here is unknown, it being yet another example of back-formation, the river being named from the place as **Bradley Brook**. Similarly local names include **Bradley Hall**, **Bradley Moor**, **Bradley Oldpark** and **Bradley Wood**. **Corley Farm**, meanwhile, stands on the land where once there was 'a woodland clearing where cranes are seen'.

Bradshaw

The only relevant record available is that of *Bradschag* in 1345, yet this is certainly 'the broad (used in the sense of extensive) grove'.

Bradway

Listed as *Bradeweye* in 1300, this is derived from the Saxon for 'broad road'. This is a fairly common definition for place-names, and although they do appear in differing forms today, this is due more to regional dialects than to the corruptions of time.

Bradwell

As with **Bradbourne** this is the '(place at) the broad stream', and is listed as *Bradewelle* in Domesday and *Bradewell* in 1230. As with so many places in the county which have only a minor brook or stream, the original name of the watercourse here is now lost in the mists of time and it bears the name of the place by the process of back-formation. Hence here we find **Bradwell Brook**, and similarly **Bradwell Dale**, **Bradwell Edge**, and **Bradwell Moor**. Other local names include **Bagshaw Cavern**, named after James Bagshaw who held this place in 1658, and **Jeffery Lane**, named after one Thomas Jeffery.

Mining in the area gave rise to a safety or hard hat introduced in the 1840s. Made in Bradwell they were known as 'Bradders'.

Brailsford

There are two places named Brailsford in the county, one near North Wingfield (appearing as *Braylesford* in 1330) and the other near Derby (listed as *Braylesford* in 1242 and, quite astonishingly considering the number of characters in the name, exactly as the modern form in Domesday). Old English *baergels* is probably the origin here, from *byrgels*, 'burial-place', used in the sense of 'tumulus', clearly located on or near a river-crossing. Locally we find the same origins for **Brailsford Bridge**, **Brailsford Green**, **Brailsford Hall** and **Brailsford Mill**. **Ednaston** was originally 'Eadnoth's farmstead'; **Fiddlers Folly** recalls former resident Anne Fiddler who lived here in 1723; and **Culland Hall** stands on land once occupied by 'Cafa's land, estate'.

Bramley (near Baslow)

Nothing to do with apples but, as seen in the record dated 1239 as *Bromleye*, derived from the Old English *brom-leah*, the '(place at) the clearing overgrown with broom'.

Brampton

Together with the local names of **Brampton East Moor** and **Brampton Hall**, this is similar in origin to **Bramley** and is 'the settlement where broom grows'. Derived from the Old English or Saxon *brom-tun*, it is recorded as *Brantune* in Domesday and *Bramton* a century later.

   Bagthorpe is a local place meaning 'Baggi's outlying farm'; **Causehouse Farm** comes from 'hall of the Caus(e) family', the earliest of whom was Robert le Caus in 1292, the latest Thomas Cawse in 1565; **Chanderhill** is from the Middle English *chauntor-hyll*, 'the hill where the chorister resides', although the first element could also be used to mean 'magician'; **Freebirch** is a very modern corruption of 'three birch trees', although the correct form was still in use until at least 1857; **Ingmanthorpe** was originally 'Ingimund's outlying farm'; **Linacre House** took its name from the area of 'cultivated land where flax grows'; **Jumble Hole** means what it seems, 'disordered'; **Kitchenflat Wood** was where wild herbs and plants were gathered; **Syda Farm** and **Sida Close** tell us of the 'extensive, spacious farm'; and the delightfully named **Pocknedge** was 'Pocka's edge of land'.

Brassington

Although found as *Branzinctun* in 1086, *Brancinton* in 1195, and *Bracynton* in 1251, these do not point to any specific origin. Normally any place-name containing the element -*ing*- would follow a personal name, for it is used to mean 'the followers or the people of'. If this is the case here, then the personal name is unknown and may have been a nickname. Another school of thought cites the origin as the Saxon *brantstig-tun*, meaning 'the settlement by the steep path'; this would fit topographically as Brassington lies on a notable incline close to **Brassington Moor**.

Near here is **Harborough Farm** (and **Rocks**); originally the name of the cave at the foot of the steep hill, it tells of 'army quarters, shelter'. The cave itself evidently offered shelter to animals long extinct in Britain, as the teeth and bones of sabre-toothed cat, hyena, bison, brown bear, Irish elk, lynx and wolf have been found here. Stone Age man also resided here, and there is evidence that the place was in continuous use from the Iron Age to post-Roman times. Indeed, Defoe documents one occasion when he met a third-generation family living there as late as the eighteenth century. **Spellow Ground Farm** comes from 'the hill where speeches are made', probably the local meeting-place. **Pinder's Rocks** recalls the residence of Jane Pinder in 1725, while John Sauchevrell was at **Sacheveral Farm** in 1437. **Clipshead Farm** is derived from the Saxon for 'farm at the cliff's head'. One local name has obvious origins, and I defy anyone not to picture the weary labourer trudging home from his labours after a seemingly endless day at **Rotton Day Nook**.

Breadsall

This rather intriguing name, also seen in **Breadsall Moor** and **Breadsall Priory**, is recorded as *aet Bregdeshale* in 1002, *Braegdesheale* in 1004, *Braideshale* in Domesday and *Breideshale* at the end of the eleventh century. Despite the personal name not being recorded, there is no doubt this is 'Braegd's halh (nook or corner of land)' – a nickname related to the Old English *braegd*, 'trick, deceit', and *braegden*, 'crafty'. (Sadly we shall never know what deed or actions earned him such a nickname.)

Breaston

Recorded as *Braidestune* in 1086, *Breydiston* in 1242 and *Breydistone* in 1282, the origin here is 'Braegd's tun or settlement' (*see* Breadsall).

Bretby

Derbyshire was divided by the poorly defined boundary between those parts of England to the south and west under Saxon rule and the area under Scandinavian influence to the north and east. This divide is reflected in the origins of the place-names, with Bretby being a good example.

Recorded as *Bretebi*, *Brettebi* and *Bretteby* between 1086 and 1202, this is 'the by of the Britons'. The suffix is the Old Scandinavian *by*, which is the equivalent of the Saxon *tun*, 'farm, village, settlement', also used in the local names **Bretby Castle**, **Bretby Hall**, **Bretby Lane**, **Bretby Mill**, **Bretby Mount** and **Bretby Park**. The reference to Britons tells us this place was inhabited by Celts, or perhaps more correctly by a Romano-British community, the descendants of the earlier age in England when Celts and Romans lived in harmony.

Brizlincote Hall was built on land known as 'the forest enclosure', and its name is derived from later Middle English which, except for the vagaries of pronunciation and the accents of the speakers, would be largely understood by a twenty-first-century time traveller.

Bretton

The significant records here are of *Brettone* in 1240 and *Brecton* in 1301, both of which may point to the true origins. The former suggests the Old English *bretta-tun*, 'the settlement of the Britons' (*see* Bretby), while the *-ct-*, if correct, leads to *brect-tun*, 'the settlement on the brook', from the same tongue.

The **Barrell Inn** is one of the many names derived from the signs, which evolved from the simplest ale stakes discussed in the introduction. This inn is one of the highest in England, standing 1,200 feet above sea-level.

Brimington

As discussed under **Brassington**, the element *-ing-* is usually indicative of a personal name. Listed as *Brimintune* in Domesday, *Brumingeton* in 1183, *Bremiton* in 1197 and *Brimentone* in 1230, this is a Saxon or Old English name meaning 'the settlement of the people or followers of Breme'.

Brock Hill comes from 'the hill where badger setts are found'; **Dixon's Lock** was held by James Dixon in 1846; **Hazard's Cottage** was the property of James Thomas Hazard in 1895; and **Wheeldonmill Lock** was occupied by Ralph Wildon in 1632.

Brough

In 1165 we find this place as *Burgus*, while the 1253 record of *Burg* is the correct Saxon word for a 'fortified place', referring specifically to an already ancient site. **Bathamgate** is an old road which ran from Brough to Buxton; it is recorded as the *Bathum road*, clearly a reference to the waters at Buxton.

Doctor's Gate follows the route of a Roman road from Brough to Melandra Castle. It is recorded as being named after a Dr Talbot, although nothing more is known about the man.

Broughton

There are two Broughtons in Derbyshire, both having identical origins. Church Broughton was the original settlement (*see* separate entry), its name derived from the Old English *broc-tun*, 'the settlement on the brook'. Later Broughton developed nearby. Initially no more than an outlying agricultural settlement of Church Broughton, it was recorded as *Parva Broctona* ('Little Brocton'). The additions of both are of obvious origin and are comparatively recent.

Near Church Broughton we find **Sapperton**, which refers to 'the family of soap-makers'. Whether they made soap as a sideline at the farm, which seems unlikely, or if one or more of the family previously produced this commodity is not clear. At first sight the name **Ammasonfield** seems fairly complex, and yet early records show this was originally simply 'the hammer-shaped copse'.

Brushfield

With early listings as *Brichthicesfel* and *Brittrichisfield* this is 'Beorhtric's feld', the name also used locally for **Brushfield Hough**. The Saxon *feld* should not be confused with the modern field, although they had identical origins and were used in much the same way. The Saxon version referred to an open tract of land which had been deliberately cleared of trees and similar growth.

Bubnell

Recorded in Domesday as *Bubenenle* and as *Bobenhull* in 1238, this is the '(place at) Bubba's hill'. Bubba is a personal name commonly found in place-names.

Bugsworth

This name appears as *Buggisworth, Bougesworth* and *Buggesword* in 1275, 1285 and 1315 respectively, and such variations over a period of just forty years seem to suggest there must have been an earlier, unknown, name (probably markedly different from any of the three given above). Having no records of this earlier name, we are forced to attempt to define the name with what we have. The first element is thought to be the Old English personal name Buduc suffixed by the Saxon *worth*, used here in the sense of 'homestead'.

Bupton

As discussed under Bubnell, the personal name Bubba is quite common in place-names and it is also the origin of Bupton. Indeed, the meaning is exactly the same for both Bupton and Bubnell, 'Bubba's hill', although there is no reason to believe it referred to the same person. The modern forms of the two names are rather different, and the historical records also show marked differences: Bupton appears as *Bubandun* in 1002, *Bubedune* in 1086, *Bubbendon* in 1169 and *Bubendona* in 1197.

The Angel war memorial at Buxton. (Photo: Andy Savage)

Burbage on the Wye

The listing as *Burebeche* in 1172 is the only record of note we have available, which means it is impossible to know whether the origins are 'brook of the fortified place' or 'valley of the fortified place'. A tributary of the Wye, **Burbage Brook**, takes its name from the place, although it seems likely it had an earlier, unknown, name. Burbage in Padley, listed as *Burbache* in around 1200, is exactly the same.

Nearby is **Poole's Cavern** which tradition would have us believe was the hideout of an outlaw after whom it was named. However, other than as an historical anecdote dating from the seventeenth century, there is no documented evidence to confirm this and we cannot therefore consider it to be the true origin.

Burley Hill

The name taken by back-formation to name **Burley Brook**, as well as **Burley Wood**, **Burley Grange** and **Burley Meadows**, it is listed as *Burleye* in 1251. This name comes from the Saxon *burg-leah*, the 'woodland clearing by or belonging to a fortified place'.

Burnaston

Plenty of documented forms of this place-name, including *Burnulfestune* in Domesday, *Brunolviston* in 1242, and *Brunufystone* in 1279, leave us in no doubt this is 'Brunwulf's settlement'.

Burton

One of the most common place-names in the country, Burton, as we would expect, has a very simple meaning. Derived from the Old English *burh-tun*, this is always 'the settlement by a fortified place'.

Butterley

Listings such as *Buterleg* in 1276 and *Buterleye* in 1330 confirm this is derived from the Old English for the '(place at) the woodland clearing which yields plenty of butter'.

Buxton

Early records of this well-known town include *Buchestanes* in 1100, *Bucstanes* in 1230 and *Bucstones* in 1287. At first glance we might expect the suffix to

This well in Buxton is situated at the foot of The Slopes. (Photo: Andy Savage)

come from the Saxon *-tun*, 'settlement', but Buxton emphasises the importance of examining early records, for the examples given here clearly show the suffix is actually derived from the Saxon *stan*, 'stone'. Knowing this we can discount the first element as a personal name for this is virtually unknown. Without any clues to any known Saxon word which may fit the first element here, we must compare Buxton with similar place-names where the meaning *is* known. Buckstone in Gloucestershire is known to have been named from a rocking stone which was found there. The region around Buxton certainly has enough stones, yet there is no record of a stone which may provide an explanation. The best guess we can offer to the origins of Buxton is from the Old English *bug-stan*, the '(place at) the bowing stone'.

The famous **St Anne's Well**, a source of healing waters for centuries, is in fact two wells, one producing warm waters, the other cold. The warm water well has shown no noticeable fluctuations since it was first used by the Romans; every day 200,000 gallons of water come to the surface at a constant 28 degrees Celsius.

For many years cheese and drink have been a popular combination, so it was no surprise that the **Cheshire Cheese Hotel** was chosen as a name, especially as it doubled as an appetiser to tempt in hungry passers-by. The **Eagle Hotel** may have either Christian or heraldic origins, although we would expect a 'coloured' eagle if it were the latter. **The Swan** is nearly always heraldic, and furthermore can be traced to either Henry VIII or Edward III. The **New Inn** seems obvious enough, but many such can hardly be considered 'new' today. There can hardly be a town in the Midlands which does not have a **Robin Hood Inn**, yet the majority of inn signs were never intended to portray the folk hero himself but rather a woodsman, as is the case with the **Royal Forester**. While it may seem odd to find a **Staffordshire Knot** in Derbyshire it is no real surprise, for the name does not derive from the nickname of the South Staffordshire Regiment but was part of the arms of the barons of Stafford who held land around here. The **Sun Inn** is a member of what we can call the 'welcoming' class of names, as is the **Anglers Rest** close to the River Wye.

C

Calke

Although the only surviving records are as *Calc* in 1132 and *Chalke* in 1196, we know the name dates from at least five hundred years earlier. The origin here is the Old English *calc*, 'chalk, limestone', which is thought to refer to a limestone hill.

Callow

As with other Callows in Derbyshire, this is from the Old English for the '(place at) the cold hill', and it is also taken for **Callow Carr Farm** and **Callow Park Farm**.

Stainsborough Hall takes its name from the earlier settlement of 'Steinn's fortified place' on the same site. Pitty Wood in Wirksworth gave its name to **Rough Pitty Side**, 'enclosure near a pit or hollow'.

Calow

This has a slightly different spelling from the other three Callows in Derbyshire. Given their proximity, we would expect them all to have evolved with identical spellings. However, we can be quite certain that Calow has a different origin. Recorded as *Calehale* in Domesday and *Calale* in 1279, this name has yet another origin in the Old English *calu-halh*, probably used here in the sense of 'bare spur of hill', as in the local name of **Calow Green**.

In the days when the horse was the principal means of transport, inns were the equivalent of the modern motorway service station, where the fast food and fuel of the day were beer and a blacksmith. In order to make travellers aware of the facilities available, innkeepers named their premises accordingly. The **Anvil Inn** is an occasional alternative to the more common Blacksmiths or Horseshoes.

Calton Lees

Known as Calton since at least 1330, the name is derived from the Saxon *calf-tun*, which is as it seems, 'the settlement where calves are reared'.

Calver

Similar to Calton Lees, Calver (and **Calver Peak** and **Calver Sough**) used to be a farm devoted to the rearing of cattle, the name coming from the Old English for 'the ridge where calves are grazed'. It is seen as *Caluoure* in Domesday, *Caluore* in 1199 and *Calfover* in 1239.

Carsington

Domesday's listing as *Ghersintune* is not the only example of the great work getting proper names very wrong indeed. Hence we need to examine the later records of *Kercinton* in 1251 and *Kersinton* in 1276, both of which still appear quite different from today's Carsington. However, we can be fairly certain the name takes its first element from the Saxon *caersen*, 'of cress', giving us 'the settlement where cress grows'. **Carsington Pasture** also appears on maps.

Castleton

Domesday's extended entry as *castellum Willelmi peuerel* is not much help in defining the name, although it does show today's form to be correct as 'the tun (settlement) by the castle'. The name is also recorded as **Castleton Mill** in some historical records.

Minor place-names around Castleton are numerous and diverse: **Winnats** is derived from the description of 'the pass through which the wind sweeps'; **Tricket Bridge** stands on land held by Robert Trykett from at least 1439; and **Kings Heartfall** is a clear reference to this region's history as part of the Royal Forest of the Peak, when heart- would have correctly been hart- (the male deer). **Treak Cliff** is a difficult name. It is thought to come from the Old English *trega* meaning 'pain, grief', plus *ac*, 'an oak tree', hence it may refer to 'the oak where hangings took place'.

Aside from the famous and unique **Blue John Cavern** and stone, there is also **Oclow Cavern** on 'oak tree hill'. At 200 metres this is the deepest in England and fully merits its alternative name of 'Giant's Hole'. **Windy Knoll Cave**, excavated in the 1870s, produced the largest collection of bones ever uncovered in one place in England. Some 6,800 bones and 500 teeth illustrated the fauna of the Pleistocene period, including bison, grizzly bears, wolves and the infamous sabre-toothed cat.

Catton

Records such as *Chetun* in 1086, *Catiton* in 1208 and the modern form as early as 1236 do not help to reveal if the personal name here is 'Catta or Kati's settlement'. **Catton Hall** and **Catton Wood** have the same root. Catton Hall, a simple yet attractive Georgian red-brick building, was erected in 1745 by James, Gibbs for Christopher Horton.

Chaddesden

Personal names as part of a place-name can be difficult to tie down. Chaddesden's *Cedesdene*, *Chadesdena*, *Chadesdene* and *Chaddesdene* up to the thirteenth century could either point to 'Ceadd's or Ceaddi's valley'. This name is also seen in **Chaddesden Common** and **Chaddesden Park**.

Chapel en le Frith

This small town proclaims itself the 'Capital of the Peak'. As far as the origin of the name is concerned, the only record of note dates from 1332 as *capella del Frith*. Only the last element needs to be examined, and is revealed to be derived from the Saxon *fyrhth*, giving 'the chapel in the woodland'.

Malcoff is a local name which has remained a mystery, although one offering suggests it derives from the French for 'bad cave', suggesting a dangerous pothole. However, no geological evidence for such a pothole has ever been found, and it would still be apparent even if it had been filled in. **Stodhart Farm** was the home of William le Stothird and his family from at least 1504. **Patient Dock Croft** is a track named after a plant found there, *Rumex Patentia*. **Stone**

This milestone is not as old as the lettering and weathering might suggest.

Jub Field is a reference to the shape, jub being a corruption of 'jug'. **Warmbrook Barn** is clearly 'the warm brook', although the brook is not warm in any sense. It is possible it was once fed by a warm spring, in which case we should read this as 'less cold' when compared with other watercourses nearby.

Some people may be surprised to learn there was once a close link between the church and taverns, as indicated by the religious theme of a number of pub names. One such is the **Cross Keys Inn**, which is named after the symbol of St Peter. The **Shoulder of Mutton** was often adopted by coaching inns to advertise that this dish was on the menu. Served with a cucumber sauce, it was considered a delicacy.

Charlesworth

This name is recorded as *Cheuenesuurde* in 1086, *Chauelisworth* in 1286 and *Chavelesworth* in 1290. Names with the suffix *worth*, 'enclosed settlement', invariably have a personal name as the first element. Here a nickname derived from the Old English *ceafl* meaning 'jaw' is one possibility, although the same word can also mean 'ravine'. Doubtless the name was later influenced by neighbouring Charlestown, not recorded before 1843.

Nearby **Gamesley** is a Saxon name meaning 'Gamall's clearing', while **Shittern Clough** dates from the same period and is the 'clough with a stream used as an open sewer'. **Monk's Road** recalls a time when the place was associated with the Abbey of Basingwerk. From the Old English *geolu* and the Old Scandinavian *slakki* we get 'the yellow shallow valley', a reference to the colour of either the vegetation or more likely the soil. Today this place is known by the delightful name **Yellow Slacks**.

Chatsworth

Found in Domesday as *Chetesuorde* and as *Chattesworth* in the thirteenth century, the name is derived from 'Ceatt's enclosed settlement' – the gentleman in question would doubtless be astonished at the splendour of the place today when compared with his humble settlement. Many names around the estate commemorate people and events in the history of both the nation and the family. **Queen Mary's Bower**, for example, an area which was once much closer to the site of the original house within the walled garden, is said to be where Mary, Queen of Scots took her exercise when she was a prisoner here.

Chellaston

Records show this place as *Celerdestune* in Domesday and *Chelardeston* a century later, which can only mean that the name was originally 'Ceolheard's settlement'.

The Church of St Mary and All Saints has the town's best-known feature, and contains five alabaster tombs dedicated to the Filjambe family. (Photo: Andy Savage)

Chellaston Hill

In the Middle Ages Chellaston was an important source of alabaster which craftsmen sculpted into the milky-white tombs that decorate many an English church. And not only English, for at its height in the fifteenth century Chellaston was exporting this much sought-after stone as far afield as France, Italy, Spain and even Iceland.

Chelmorton

There are plenty of examples of early forms here including *Chelmaredon* in 1196, *Chelemeredune* in 1225, *Chilmerdon* in 1236 and *Cheilmardon* in 1265, all of which show this to be the '(place at) Ceolmaer's hill', also seen on maps as **Chelmorton Flat** and **Chelmorton Low**.

Here we find **Thirst House**, or 'the giant's house', a cave where many remains have been found of both prehistoric and Roman occupation. **The Burro** is a field-name derived from the dialect *burr* which was used specifically to describe 'solid rock encountered when driving a level through soft material'.

Chesterfield

From the middle of the tenth century we find *ad Cesterfelda* which has its origins in 'the clearing by the Roman station'. Chesterfield is located on Ryknild Street, a famous Roman road.

Today it simply would not be Chesterfield without its most famous landmark of the crooked spire. Of course the question we all ask is – *why* is it crooked? Folklore, as we would expect, has the answer – to be accurate three answers, the simplest of which is a lightning strike. Another tale suggests the marriage of a virgin in the church was so astonishing that the spire twisted around to see the wonder for itself. The third and most elaborate tale concerns a magician who managed to convince a blacksmith from Bolsover that shoeing the Devil was a perfectly good idea. The understandably nervous blacksmith was shaking so much he drove one of the nails into the Devil's foot. Howling in agony, the Devil shot off over the rooftops towards Chesterfield where, as he passed the church, he lashed out in his rage, catching the spire and leaving it twisted.

The real reason the 228ft spire is twisted is largely due to an unfortunate combination of events precipitated by the decimation of local craftsmen by the Black Death around 1349. This left an inexperienced team who used too much unseasoned wood in the frame and failed to include cross-bracing to strengthen the structure. It is hardly surprising that the spire twisted under the weight of 32 tons of lead tiling!

Chesterfield Market Hall, built in 1857, revamped and reopened on 15 November 1980. (Photo: Andy Savage)

PAVEMENTS SHOPP

LIBRARY

THE MARKET

The **Barley Mow** is a simple sign from early times, where a major ingredient of beer is shown in a mow or stack. **The Barrel Inn** is another 'brewing' name. A reminder of Chesterfield's early days is seen in the **Blue Stoops**, where 'stoop' refers to a post or pillar holding up a porch. Before premises were numbered, the stoops were painted in different colours for ease of recognition. The **Crispin Inn** is named after St Crispin, the patron saint of cobblers and shoemakers; famously the Battle of Agincourt was fought on St Crispin's Day, 25 October 1415. **The Golden Fleece** may well bring to mind the Greek legend of Jason and the Argonauts, but the name is also associated with the Knights of the Golden Fleece, a chivalric order created for the protection of the church. The name probably originated from the practice of hanging a line of fleeces across a river or stream to trap any fine particles of gold which were washed down by the current. The knights' badge depicted a ram with a red band around its middle, often used today to illustrate the name on the pub sign.

The Phoenix, a fabled bird said to rise from its own ashes, was chosen as a pub name by an owner or innkeeper who had resurrected either himself or the pub so named. **The Square and Compass** is a reference to the basic tools used by carpenters, joiners and masons, and may indicate either an earlier trade of the owner or innkeeper, or that this house was popular with those in one or more of these trades. Named after the husband and consort of Queen Victoria, the **Albert Inn** recalls Francis Albert Augustus Charles Emmanuel (1819–61), the second son of Ernest I, Duke of Saxe-Coburg-Gotha, known to all as Prince Albert. Referring to the market held here for a great many years, the pub known as **The Barkers Bar** features the name given to a street seller, the same theme being followed by **The Barrow Boy**. Less immediately obvious are the origins of **The Cannon** as an heraldic sign, the image being common in the arms of the Tudor monarchs Edward VI, Mary and Elizabeth I.

Chesterfield's street-names include the obviously named **Back Lane**, recorded as **rectro manum** in 1306, and **Beetwell Street**, 'the spring of the Bete family', which was held by Rog' fil' Bete in 1278. **Broad Pavement** may be clearly descriptive but it is interesting to note that the street was known as **Narrow Lane** in 1721; perhaps the original name was coined by pedestrians while the modern one reflects the views of the road-user.

Gluman Gate is derived from 'the street of the minstrels', or medieval buskers; **Hollis Lane**s was an area held by John Holleys in 1559; **Knifesmith Gate** was the home of John le Knyfsmyth in 1371; **The Shambles**, literally 'the flesh benches', was where meat was sold in the market, usually at a spot that remained in shade for much of the day to help prevent the goods from spoiling; and **Souter Row** is from the Old English *sutere raw*, 'the street of the shoemaker(s)'.

Stonegravels is a simple name to define, being the '(place at) the stone quarry', although which stone was taken (and what it was used for) is not known. **Spital**, as with all such-named places throughout the country, is a shortened form of 'hospital', and here refers to the Leper Hospital of St Leonard, the earliest reference to which is as *fratribus leprosis de Cestrefeld*.

Chinley

Recorded as *Chineleia* in 1200 and *Chinlegh* in 1286, the name comes from 'the clearing by a ravine'.

Past residents are remembered in local names including **Bennett Barn**, after William Bennitt who lived here in 1603; **Brierly Green**, in honour of George Brearly, documented as being here in 1597; and **Carrington House**, the home of James Carrington by 1624.

Chisworth

Listed as *Chiseuurde* by Domesday and *Chissewrde* at the end of the twelfth century, the name comes from the Saxon and means 'Cissa's enclosed settlement'.

Chunal

Recorded as *Ceolhal* in Domesday and *Chelhala* in 1185 this name derives from the Saxon for 'Ceola's nook of land'.

The **Grouse Inn** certainly had its origins in the bird, but it was more likely to have been the meeting-place of gamekeepers or beaters than an indication of the menu. In more recent times, when sign painters began to look for original ways to portray common names, the alternative meaning of 'grumble' was introduced. This latter usage began in the nineteenth century as soldiers' slang, and the only etymological link between the two meanings is as a pub name.

Church Broughton

Church Broughton was the original settlement here (*see* Broughton), appearing as *Broctune* and *Brocton* in the eleventh and thirteenth centuries respectively. The name is from the Old English *broc-tun*, 'the settlement on the brook'. *Clifton Cliptune* in Domesday and *Clyfton* in 1221 enable us to define this as 'the settlement on a hill or hill slope on the brink of a river'.

An ancient pub name, the **Cock Inn** became increasingly popular during the seventeenth century through 'cock-ale', a mixture of ale, the jelly of a boiled cockerel and other ingredients.

Clowne

This name was recorded as *Clune* in 1002. There was formerly a Clun in Nottinghamshire, near Carburton on the River Poulter. Clun may well be an old river-name, identical with the same name found in Shropshire. Hence we can assume it must be a former name for the Poulter. Clumber is a place on the Poulter at the foot of a hilly region and can be seen to contain the original river-name Clun and the Welsh *bre*, meaning 'hill'. It is easy to see how Clowne is merely a corruption of Clun, the watercourse being an arm of the Poulter.

Harlesthorpe has its origins in a Scandinavian personal name and means 'Thoraldr's outlying farm', while **Rameley Hall** can still be seen today as the '(place at) the large, spacious woodland clearing'.

Coal Aston

As with other Astons in Derbyshire and elsewhere in England, this is 'the eastern tun (settlement)'. Here the prefix is a corruption of 'cold' (a common error), as seen by the listing in 1260 as *Cold Aston*.

The Cross Daggers public house is named from the emblem of the Hallamshire Cutlers Company, presumably once the trade of an early landlord or owner.

Coddington

As seen by *Codintone* in 1219 and *Codington* in 1246, this was once 'Codda's settlement'.

Codnor

There can be no doubt that this was 'Codda's ridge', as evidenced by Domesday's *Cotenovre* and *Codenoura* a century later.

The Miners Arms marks the importance of mining to the area, while **Bostock Yard** remembers a local family who owned not only their own farm but their own slaughterhouse. One family member, the enterprising William Bostock, is recorded as being not only a farmer, but also a road surveyor and cemetery keeper in a document dating from the latter half of the nineteenth century. **Glasshouse Hill** is a road where the **Glasshouse Inn** stood at the time of the Pentrich Rebellion in 1817. The rebels stopped at the inn on the way to Nottingham, but they never completed their journey. Detained by the authorities of the day, the men were sent to trial. The three leaders – Jeremiah Brandeth, Isaac Ludlam and William Turner – were the last men to be

The New Clock Inn at Codnor.

sentenced to be hanged, drawn and quartered, with the vast majority of their supporters being transported to penal colonies around the British Empire. The table used for the executions was later moved to Derby Museum.

Finally there is **Thomson Drive**, named after George Thomson, the village doctor from 1901. He served the community in many ways, besides being the local physician, until he retired in the 1940s. He is also recorded as the first person in Codnor to own a motor car.

Combs

Early records differ little from the modern form, appearing as *Comb* in 1169 and *Combes* in 1374. This is the plural of the Old English *camb*, 'comb, crest of a hill'. The place is located on the slope of the hill known as **Black Edge**.

Conksbury

Records such as *Cranchesberie* in 1086, *Cankersburia* in 1318, and *Conkesburgh* in 1339 all point to the Old English *cranuces burg*, meaning 'fortified place where cranes are found'.

The Shoulder of Mutton Inn. Shoulder was a delicacy in coaching days.

Coton in the Elms

Recorded as *Cotune* in Domesday and *Cotene* in 1242, this 'cottage settlement among the elm trees' did not gain its addition until comparatively recently.

Cotton

The origins here are from 'Codda's settlement', as indicated by the early records of *Codetune* in 1086 and *Codinton* in 1194.

Cowdale

This place near Buxton is listed as *Cudala* at the end of the twelfth century. There can be no doubt that it is what it seems, the '(place at) the valley of the cows'.

Cowley

There are two Cowleys within Derbyshire. The one near Winster is recorded as *Collei* in the eleventh century, while the other at Dronfield is listed as *College* in 1315. Both are derived from the Saxon *col-leah*, meaning 'woodland clearing where charcoal is burnt'.

Cresswell

In 1176 this place was recorded as *Cressewella*, which is derived from the '(place at) the stream where watercress grows'.

The caves of **Cresswell Crags** (along with Kent's Cavern in Torquay) are regarded as the earliest authenticated sites of human habitation in England.

Crewton

A place-name coined long after the Saxon era, this place is named after a family named Crewe.

Crich

The home of the National Tramway Museum is found as *Cryc* in 1009, *Crice* in 1086, *Cruc* in 1166, *Cruch* in the late twelfth century and *Cruz* in 1229. Crich is derived from the British or Celtic *cruc*, meaning simply 'a hill', the hill in question being known as **Cruchill** today. Local names of similar origin include **Crich Carr**, **Crich Chase**, **Crich Cliff** and **Crich Common**. There is also a **Cliff Inn** here.

Hereabouts we find 'Coda's farm' has evolved to become **Coddington**; **Plaistow** is the 'place where people met for recreation'; **Shuckstonefield** is derived from 'demon's or goblin's thornbush'; and a Danish personal name is seen in **Thurlowbooth**, from 'Thurlak's temporary shelter'.

Cromford

This is listed as *Crunforde* in Domesday, *Crumford* in 1204 and *Crumbeford* in 1251. The first element is derived from the Old English *crumb*, meaning 'crooked'. The place-name can be defined as 'the ford by a bend', which crosses the Derwent. Local names spawned from the name include **Cromford Bridge**, **Cromford Mill**, **Cromford Moor** and **Cromfordhill**.

Barrel Edge is a corruption of its origins from 'boar hill', while **Gratton's Parlour** recalls the family of William Gratton, who lived here in 1857. The Gratton family were not prominent in Cromford but were very much so in the neighbouring Wirksworth parish.

Crowdicote

Listings of this name include *Crudecote* in 1223, *Croudecote* in 1251 and as *Welleton Cruddecote* in 1287, which leads us to the definition of 'Cruda's cottage'. The late thirteenth-century record as Welleton probably refers to an outlying settlement which was later either abandoned or swallowed up as the larger settlement expanded.

Dating from the days when the horse was the only mode of transport available, the **Pack Horse Inn** would have offered travellers the chance of a fresh mount.

Cubley

Cobelei in Domesday, *Cubbeleg* in 1232 and *Cubbelegh* in 1255 all point to the origin of this place as 'Cubba's woodland clearing'. **Cubley Carr**, **Cubley Common**, **Cubley Covert**, **Cubley Lodge**, **Cubley Mill**, **Cubley Park** and **Cubleywood Farm** were all named from the main place.

Curbar

Early records of this name are many and varied. *Cordeburg* in 1203, *Cordesburwe* in 1285, *Quordborough* in 1346, *Cordborgh* in 1356, *Corburg* in 1365, *Coresburgh* in 1423, and *Corber* in 1577 all point to this originally being 'Corda's fortified place'. Despite the many records available the personal name here cannot be stated with absolute certainty, for there are a number of possible names which could fit.

Minor names in the locality include **Grislow Field**, derived from the Saxon describing 'gristly open land'; even today the soil is thin with rocks strewn around. **Hearthstone Field** is aptly named for this would have been where such rocks were obtained for the hearth; stones of the right size and shape occur naturally here.

D

Dalbury

With records as *Dellingberie*, *Dalebir* and *Dalenburi* in the eleventh century, we can be certain this was 'the fortified place of Dealla's people'. Furthermore, we also know that Dealla was the name of a moneyer, corresponding to the Old High German *Tallo*. Both have a common root which is represented in Old English by *deall*, meaning 'proud, resplendent'. As early as 990 the place is referred to as *Cynedealle rod*, with documented details about a woman named Cynedeall. It is tempting to suggest that this woman was the proud one referred to in the name.

Personal names deriving from a person's trade or skill were not as common as they are today, although it is quite possible that many personal names are simply not recognised as such.

The **Black Cow** is an heraldic pub name, taken from the coat of arms of a local family, landowner or trade. As with so many names on this theme, the origins remain unknown.

Dale Abbey

Today the name simply means 'the dale', with the addition being obvious. A record dating from 1242 as *La Dale* confirms this, although if we go back to the previous century we find it listed in 1158 as *Depedala*, which can be clearly seen to be 'the deep dale'. **Dale Moor** evolved alongside the main name.

Boyah Grange is an unusual minor place-name derived from 'Boie's enclosure'.

Darley

There are two Darleys in Derbyshire, both having the same meaning, derived from the Old English *deor-leah*, 'the wood frequented by deer'. The place near Bakewell is recorded as *Dereleie* in 1086, *Derleia* in 1125 and *Derlega* in 1155, while the place now known as Darley Abbey (near Derby) is found as *Derlega* in 1199, *Derleg* in 1212 and *Derley* in 1230. While the addition requires no explanation, it is logical to find one of them carrying an identifying second part. It should also be noted that the Saxon *deor* is used to mean 'animals' as well as specifically 'deer'. Therefore although the two definitions have been said to be identical, it may be that one (or even both) actually refers to animals other than deer.

Near Darley are several minor names of interest including **Fallinge**, which comes from the Old English *faelging*, meaning 'the fallow's land'. Standing on the boundary between the parishes of Darley and Matlock, as well as between the ancient Hundreds of High Peak and Wirksworth, is **Morledge Farm**, so it is no surprise that the watercourse from which the name is taken means 'boundary stream'. **Sydnope Hall** occupies an area known to the Saxons as the '(place) at the broad valley'.

The seemingly impossible name of **Hanging Holes** is derived from the Old English *hangende-hol*, 'the sloping hollow'. **Knab Hall** was built near 'the knoll', and **Siberia Nursery** has one of the 'far-flung' names given somewhat sarcastically to places on the furthest boundaries of the parish.

The Abbey public house occupies part of the original twelfth-century abbey, most of which was destroyed by Henry VIII during the Dissolution. The village of Darley Abbey began life as an eighteenth-century cotton mill village when Thomas Evans built his own mill there in 1783. His family's domination of village life continued for many years, as shown by the 1841 census; of a total population of 1,059, 750 worked in the Evanses' cotton mill and another 80 in their paper mill. This must surely mean that almost everyone of working age was in the family's employ. Sadly the resident line ended with the passing of Ada Evans in 1929.

Denby

Recorded as *Denebi* in Domesday and *Deneby* in 1234, the name comes from the Old Scandinavian meaning 'the village of the Danes'.

Local names include **Denby Bottles**, **Denby Car**, **Denby Common**, **Denby Dam** and **Denby Old Hall**, all of identical origin. **Godber's Lum** features the Saxon element *lum*, 'a pool', which was the property of Samuel Godber in 1783. There is also **Salter Wood**, which refers to 'salt-seller's wood' (not to be confused with a salt cellar!).

Derby

Said to be home to the finest Georgian church in England, the city of Derby can also boast the first public park in England, the Arboretum, which opened in 1840. It was also the site of the earliest market charter to be granted in England, by Henry II in 1154. As a place-name the Old Scandinavian *diurby* or *diuraby* can be seen in the records as *Deoraby* in 917 and *Deorby* in 959, while the modern form is found in the Domesday record of 1086. Thus we are able to define the place-name as 'the village where deer are seen'. There is also a listing as *Nordworthig* in 1000. Although there can be no doubt this refers to the same place it cannot be seen as an alternative name, and probably refers to an outlying region which was swallowed up by the expansion of Derby itself many years ago.

The **Bell & Castle Inn** is a very old pub name. Many 'Bell & . . .' names are remnants of a time when it was common practice to combine two taverns when there was insufficient trade to sustain both premises. The bell can also be seen to have religious connections and is said to 'speak all languages'; furthermore it is an easily recognisable shape and is comparatively easy to reproduce. The name of the **Blessington Carriage** was taken at random from a book examining the days of coaching. This particular coach belonged to Margaret, Countess of Blessington (1789–1849), a woman noted for her beauty and remembered for several published works, including *Conversations with Lord Byron* (1832). As with all 'colour/animal' pub names, **The Blue Dog** was once owned by the Manners family of Grantham, Lincolnshire. They owned several inns, all of which they renamed using the prefix 'Blue' to show their political allegiance to the Whigs. One of Shakespeare's most popular and endearing characters is recalled by **The Falstaff**. The **Brick and Tile** is clearly a reference to the building trade, the intention being to attract such workers. While the **Drill Hall Vaults** has military origins, the **Mafeking Hotel** is a reference to the 217-day siege of Mafeking in South Africa, relieved in 1900.

Not every word is used today in its original sense. The **Grange Inn**, for example, may conjure up images of a green haven, either natural or man-made, but originally it was used to mean a 'granary', and indeed some signs depict a farm bailiff (or granger) overseeing grain being loaded into a huge wooden storage vat.

The **Brunswick Inn** is named after the Duke of Brunswick, who was resident in England for many years before being fatally wounded at the Battle of Waterloo while fighting on the side of the British forces. The **Buck in the Park** is a superbly simple reflection of Derby's coat of arms, which depicts a hart on a green base; the pub sign shows an antlered stag on a grassy mound. **The Byron** is a tribute to the poet Lord Byron. The **Castle & Falcon** comes from the coat of arms of the family of Catherine Parr, the last of Henry VIII's six wives.

The **Durham Ox** was named after a famous animal bred by Charles Collings of Ketton near Darlington. At six years old this beast weighed 2 tons and its owner, who had paid the enormous sum of £250 for the animal, made a substantial profit by touring the country with his prized possession in the early nineteenth century, with a specially constructed vehicle for the animal. The tremendous impression the animal made is reflected in the number of pubs named after it across the country.

The **Exeter Arms** was named after the Marquess of Exeter, who, as Donald Finley, brought home a gold medal from the 1928 Olympics in Amsterdam.

Derby Cathedral from Iron Gate. (Photo: Andy Savage)

The **Flamingo & Firkin** belongs to the Firkin Brewery, which takes its name from a small cask equivalent to a quarter of a barrel in volume. This is one of their many pubs around the country, all of which have the first element beginning with F (or sometimes Ph). The **Flower Pot** is a religious name dating from Puritan times, when the sign always depicted a flower pot containing lilies, representative of the Virgin Mary.

Bold Lane is a nineteenth-century corruption of 'Bolt', another word for an arrow, and probably refers to a maker of arrows who lived here. Another corrupted street-name is **Jury Lane**, which was once the home of the local community of Jews. **Walker Lane** recalls someone employed in cloth-making to 'walk' upon the new woollen cloth to clean it during the fulling process. The street-name probably refers to a former factory, rather than being taken from the surname of someone who was employed there. Conversely **Parcel Terrace** is nothing to do with any trade, but is derived from the old field-name for this area, telling simply of 'the piece of land'. **St Mary's Gate** was home to St Mary's Church, mentioned in Domesday but now a lost parish, although it is unclear just when (or why) it ceased to exist. In 1588 **St Mary's Bridge** witnessed the gruesome murder of three Catholic priests. As a warning to others, the perpetrators severed the arms from the bodies and displayed them on the bridge.

Hill Street is of obvious derivation, as was the former name of **Cuckold's Street** – sadly there is no evidence to point to specific people and/or events here.

Around the city we find minor names such as **Cowsley**, 'Colle's woodland clearing'; **Little Chester**, 'the Roman camp', with the prefix differentiating it from the city in Cheshire; **Morledge** tells us this place stood on 'the boundary stream'; **Rowditch** was the '(place at) the rough ditch'; **Siddals** is named from 'the broad corner of land'; and **Chequers Lane** ran alongside a field with a naturally checkered appearance.

Derbyshire

There is no need to redefine the name discussed at length under the county town, but we should note that records include *Deorbyscir* in 1049 and Derbyscire in Domesday.

Derbyshire today reflects the north–south divide in England, not only in its speech but also in the scenery, which changes dramatically from the industrial south and west to the highlands of the north and east. This divide can be seen in the archaeological record too. The upland farmers of the Bronze Age were closely related to those of Cumbria, Cornwall, Wales and Scotland, while the people of the south and west can be traced to groups who migrated along the river valleys from lowland areas through the pottery remains found in both regions.

Visitors to the county pass signs telling them they are entering the Peak National Forest, but there is no observable difference in the number of trees.

The loss of so much of the 'forest' can be proved by a glance at Domesday, which records that over one-third of the county was covered in woodland. Nine hundred years later trees covered just 4 per cent, which is less than the 6 per cent of the national average and explains why drivers cannot see the wood OR the trees. Further evidence of the degree of deforestation in Derbyshire is given by the number of place-names ending in -leah, meaning 'clearing', showing just how many of the county's settlements started life in a natural glade among the trunks of long-established trees.

Derbyshire may no longer have many of its trees, but mining has left its mark on the landscape during the last two millennia or more. It has been estimated that between 50,000 and 100,000 shafts were sunk to extract ores and minerals, not all of which have yet been made safe to protect the unwary from falling in.

Derwent, River

As with many river-names (especially of major watercourses) this is a remnant of the British or Celtic language used in England before the arrival of the Romans over 2,000 years ago. Flowing for 66 miles from its source to its confluence with the Trent at Shardlow, it is recorded as *Deorwentan* and *Derwenta* and comes from the British name *Derventio*, which is also found as a place-name on the Yorkshire Derwent. It is derived from *derva*, meaning 'oak' (also seen as Welsh *derw*). Thus the river-name can be defined as 'the river where oaks are common'. The name was transferred to the village and its attendant minor names such as **Derwent Edge** and **Derwent Moor**.

The river may have followed almost the same course since the end of the last Ice Age, but it certainly has not flowed at the same rate. Even in the last fifty years the amount of water passing over Longbridge Weir at Derby has varied considerably. The weir, constructed specifically to measure the amount of water in the Derwent, saw an all-time low in the summer of 1959 of just 640 gallons per second. This may still seem a large volume of water, until it is compared with the highest recorded volume, on 10 December 1965, when an unimaginable 80,000 gallons of water gushed past every second.

Local names which merit a mention include **Cutthroat Bridge** which, while of obvious derivation, has yet to be linked to a specific incident. A record from 1635 tells how the writer found a man with a throat wound and carried him to his home at the Lady Bower, half a mile from Clough. While the writer makes no mention of the location, the current bridge is at the foot of Highshaw Clough. Whether this narrative can be accepted as evidence for the origins of the name depends on whether this was an isolated attack, in which case it seems unlikely, unless the injured man held an important office.

Ding Bank is derived from the Old Scandinavian *dyngja*, 'dung, dung-heap', used here in the sense of 'well-manured bank'. **Shireowlers** is an interesting name, albeit the place itself is now lost beneath the waters of the reservoir. Close to the border with neighbouring Yorkshire, the name recalls the 'boundary alders' marking the division and possibly planted specifically for the purpose. **Hordron Edge** is from the Old English *hord-aern*, meaning 'a store house', while **Lost Lad** is not the pub name it seems to be, but a corrupted Saxon name for 'landlord's seat hill', with *sceat* referring to a 'projecting piece of land'.

Dethick

Occasionally a place-name gives us not just a meaning but also a glimpse of the life of the community that lived there. This is the case at Dethick. Recorded as *Dethek* in 1200 and *Dethic* in 1290, the name is derived from Old English *death-ac*, literally 'death oak', giving the '(place at) the oak on which felons were hanged'. Dethick is close to Matlock, or 'the oak at which moots (meetings) are held'.

One of Dethick's less auspicious claims to fame is as the birthplace of Anthony Babbington in 1561. After the exposure of the 'Babbington Plot' to release Mary, Queen of Scots from her imprisonment at Wingfield Manor, Babbington was executed in 1586 at Tyburn.

Gregory Dam (and **Spring**) are named after former resident Rebecca Gregory, while **Holloways** refers to the 'hollow roads' – the plural is recorded too often for it to be erroneous.

Dinting

Recorded as *Dentic* in Domesday and *Duntinge* in 1226, it is thought to be derived from a British or Celtic word related to the Old Irish *dinn* and Old Norse *tindr*, meaning 'point, crag', and referring to the '(place at) the hill'. The suffix *-ing* may well indicate an unknown form which spoke of 'the people of (the place at) the hill'.

Dore

Recorded as *Dor* in 942 and in the modern form in Domesday, this is derived from the Old English *dor*, meaning 'door' in the sense of 'pass'. The name was also adopted at the local sites of **Dore Hall** and **Dore Moor**. Dore lies on a pass on the ancient boundary between the Anglo-Saxon kingdoms of Northumbria and Mercia, which was later to become the boundary between Yorkshire and Derbyshire. Its connection to Yorkshire is further emphasised by **Whirlow Wheel**, named from Whirlow in the West Riding.

Dove

This well-known river's name is derived from the British or Celtic word *dubo* (related to Welsh *du*) meaning 'black, dark'. The popular beauty spot of **Dovedale** (given as *Duuedale* in 1296) is named from the river.

Doveridge

As with Dovedale, this place is named from the River Dove. Seen as *Dubrige* in Domesday, *Duvebrug* in 1275 and *Duvebrigg* in 1330, this is the '(place at) the bridge over the River Dove'. Local names include **Doveridge Hall** and **Doveridge Woodhouse**. Here, too, is **Sedsall**, which can be defined as the '(place at) Secg's willow', and **The Dimble**, which is from the Old English *dumbel*, 'hollow (literally dimpled land)'.

The **Cavendish Arms** comes from the family name of the Dukes of Devonshire who reside at nearby Chatsworth.

Drakelow

Listed as *aet Dracan hlawen* in 942, *Drachelawe* in 1086 and *Drakelawe* in 1175, this is taken from the Saxon *dracan-hlaw*, meaning 'the dragon's mound'. A legend about a dragon was once told about this place. One wonders if it produced as much smoke as the power station cooling towers built here in the twentieth century.

Draycott

Not an uncommon minor place-name, this is derived from the Old English *draeg* and Old Scandinavian *drag*, which are never found in independent use but are only used in place-names. The word refers to a 'portage', that is a place where boats were transported overland – either to avoid a hazard, or as a short cut, or to cross from one navigable river system to another. Here the second element is the Saxon *cot*, giving 'the cottage(s) by the portage'. Later modes of transport are recalled by the **Coach & Horses**, an inn which may well have served as a stopping-place on one of the coaching routes. Nearby is **Church Wilne**, which comes from the Saxon and means the '(place at) the willow copse with a church'.

Dronfield

Appearing in ancient documents as *Dranefield* and *Dronefeld*, this is of Saxon origins as 'the clearing frequented by drones (bees)'.

It is worthwhile looking at the origins of the pub sign in order to see the beginnings of names such as the **Ash Tree**. Early signs were simply indications to travellers that refreshment was available within. In times when the vast majority of the population was illiterate, the most common sign was simply a sheaf of barley tied to what became known as an ale stake, and the 'stake' was just as likely to be a roadside tree as a man-made post or pole. Clearly from a distance the tree was easier to see than the rudimentary sign attached to it, so it is no surprise to find so many tree names used for pubs. Furthermore, in later years when sign painters were employed to produce ever more eye-catching enticements to potential customers, the tree was a fairly simple image to reproduce.

Although the image on the sign invariably depicts the mythical beast slain by St George, the **Green Dragon Inn** is actually an heraldic reference to the Earls of Pembroke. The **Heart of Oak** is a reference to ship-building; oaks were much sought-after for their centres contain no sap. Nelson's fleet, for example, featured seventy-four warships, each of which required some 2,000 trees – mostly oaks – to be felled.

The **Hyde Park Inn** can be attributed to the London park. When the original owner first heard that a licence had been granted he was staying near that park, which in turn got its name as it originally consisted of a hide of land. A hide was not a precise measurement of area but a reference to the land's rating for tax purposes, and could range from 120 to 240 acres depending on the quality. 'Invitational' pub names are quite common; sometimes a warm welcome could be suggested simply by prefixing the name with 'Jolly', as in the case of **The Jolly Farmer**, where the landlord's former occupation or that of his customers is represented. **The Old Sidings** is a pub name which speaks of its location alongside the railway, and it was probably a favourite haunt of the workmen in the yard.

Dronfield's local place-names include **Eldon Croft**, which is a slight corruption of the original 'Elton', a prominent family in the region by 1561. **Fanshaw Bank** is named after former resident Thomas Fanshawe, who is recorded here in 1636. **Quoit Green** is a somewhat unexpected corruption of the original Saxon *cot-grene*, which tells of 'the cottages on the green'; **Quoit Lane** runs right past this place. **Cally White Lane** is recorded as a lane called *Causin White* in 1669, but we have no clues as to who this person was. Lastly there is **Soaper Lane**, which took its name from an earlier farm here and means 'soap-maker' – probably an indication of the former trade of the farmer rather than indicating that soap was actually made here.

Duckmanton

Although we have found listings such as *Ducemannestun* in 1002, *Dochemanesun* in Domesday and *Duchemanetun* in 1160, the personal name here is by no means certain but the meaning is probably something akin to 'Duceman's settlement'.

On the Chesterfield Road is the **Arkwright Arms**, which is named in honour of Sir Richard Arkwright (1732–98), the man who invented the first cotton-spinning frame. In 1771 he erected the first spinning-mill driven by water power and is justly remembered as a pioneer of the factory system.

Duffield

'The (place at) the woodland clearing frequented by doves', as seen in the Domesday record of *Duuelle*, and later listings as *Duffelda* and *Duffeld*, together with records of the local names **Duffield Bridge**, **Duffield Hall** and **Duffieldbank**. **Burley** is from the Old English *burgh-leah*, which tells us this was 'the woodland clearing near or held by a fortified place'. A much less complex definition is found for **Cumber Hill** from '(the place at) Cumbra's hill', while **Turpins** recalls the family of Francisca Turping who were here in 1598 and probably much earlier.

The Patten Makers Arms celebrates the people who made pattens, an early version of galoshes. They consisted of a thick wooden sole mounted on an oval iron ring and enabled pedestrians to walk clear of the mud and filth which covered most of the streets in towns. The footwear gave rise to the expression 'to run on pattens', meaning to talk a lot or make a lot of noise, as the wearers of pattens most certainly did.

Dunston

Dunestune, *Dunnestona* and *Dunnestun* all show this place-name to be derived from 'Dunn's tun or settlement'.

E

Eaton

There are two Eatons in Derbyshire, Little Eaton (seen as *Detton* in Domesday and *Lytyll Eton* in 1502), and Cold Eaton (*Eitune* in Domesday, *Eyton* in 1251 and *Coldeyton* in 1323). Eaton is derived from the Saxon *eg-tun*, 'the settlement on an island'. It should be noted that 'island' can also refer to land partly enclosed by a bend in a river, or comparatively dry land in marshy ground (perhaps even seasonal marshland). The additions are self-explanatory.

Eckington

The place-name is recorded as *Eccingtun* in 1002, *Echintune* in 1086 and *Ekinton* in 1194, which is evidence of the Saxon origins for 'the settlement of the followers or people of Ecca'. Local names with the same derivation include **Eckington Park**, **Eckington Leas**, **Eckington Marsh** and **Eckington Hall**.

The Butchers Arms near Eckington has a modern sign, although the name could refer to the former trade of an early owner or innkeeper.

The war memorial at Marsh Lane, near Eckington, is dedicated to local people who lost their lives in the two world wars.

Other local names worthy of mention include **Troway**, from the Old English *trog-weg*, 'trough or valley road'. **Field's Wheel** was home to Michael Field in 1780; **Geer Lane** was held by Thomas Gere of Beighton; **Renishaw** is derived from 'Reynold's copse'; **Setcup Lane** ran towards 'the seat-shaped hill'; and **Sloadlane** features the Saxon element *slaed*, meaning 'valley'. Lastly **Neverfear Dam** is a fairly modern name chosen for effect alone and has no etymological reasoning behind it whatsoever.

Edale

Despite records of *Aidele* in Domesday, *Eydale* in 1305 and the modern form as early as 1362, it is difficult to ascertain whether the origins are Saxon *eg-dael*, the '(place at) the island valley', or Saxon *ea-dael*, '(place at) the valley of the river'. **Edale Cross**, **Edale End**, **Edale Head** and **Edale Rocks** are among the local names of similar derivation.

That mining was important in this area is reflected in the place-names. **Jaggers Clough** comes from a lead-mining dialect word: the jagger was the man in charge of the jagging horses used to carry the ore from the mine, after it had been cleaned and dressed, to the smelting mill. The earliest record of the word is dated 1306 and tells of a Thomas le Jager de parva Longesdon. **Woolpacks** is a simpler field-name, describing the shape of the rocks seen there, while **Tags Naze** tells us this was once the '(place at) Tag's headland'.

Edensor

Early listings such as *Ednesovre, Ednesouria* and *Ednesofre* show the second element here to be the Old English *ofer* preceded by a personal name giving 'Eden's bank'.

Edensor's local names include **Lindup Wood**, from the Saxon describing the 'lime tree valley'. **Moatless Plantation** may seem to have an obvious, if somewhat unusual, first element. However, the modern form is a corruption of the true origins from the Saxon *mot hlaw*, 'meeting-place hill'. **Russian Cottage** is so named as it was built in 1855 after the Duke of Devonshire received a model of a Russian farm from Tsar Nicholas I.

Edlaston

Domesday's *Ednodestun* would be quite misleading were it not for further evidence from 1229 as *Edulveston* showing this place to be 'Eadwulf's settlement'.

The farming community has been the single most important resource for most of this country's history, so it is no surprise that so many pubs celebrate agriculture in names such as **The Shire Horse**.

Ednaston

The similarity with Edlaston is not a recent phenomenon. Early records show the personal names also to be alike, as this is 'Eadnoth's settlement'.

Ednaston Lodge was the birthplace of five children, four of whom went on to become writers. Their father was the Revd C.F. Powys who left for Dorchester in 1885. His most prolific son was John Cowper Powys, but his brothers Lyttleton, Llewelyn and Theodore all published works in their adult life.

Egginton

Found as *Eghintune* in Domesday, *Eggenton* in 1242 and *Eginton* in 1228, the name is of Saxon origin as 'the settlement of the followers or the people of Ecga'. **Egginton Cottage** and **Egginton Hall** have identical origins, while **Egginton Brook** is another example of a watercourse adopting the place-name. **Hinkinhill** the is a local name derived from the 'hill shaped like an ink-horn (a variety of fungus)', while **Monk's Bridge** was built on the instructions of Burton Abbey.

Elmton

This would seem to be 'the settlement where elm trees grow', which is confirmed by the eleventh- and twelfth-century records of *Helmetune*, *Helmeton*, *Elmeton* and *Elmenton*, and is the clear basis for the local names of **Elmton Common End**, **Elmton Green** and **Elmton Park**.

As its name suggests, **Markland Farm** stands on the boundary between the parishes of **Elmton and Whitewell**, while **Markland Grips** features the dialect word *grip* from the Old English *grype* meaning 'small drain'. **Bullivants Wood** was held by John Bullivant in 1534.

Elton

Recorded as *Eltune* in Domesday, the modern form is seen as early as 1282. There can be no doubt this is 'Ella's settlement'.

Coast Rake Mine is derived from the Old English *cost-rake*, 'examination', giving the 'trial lead mine'. Landowners of the past are remembered by **Allsop Barn** and **Barker Barn** named after Robert Alsop (1829) and Samuel Barker (1734) respectively.

Elvaston

Although we have a better chance of defining a name if there are plenty of early examples, sometimes there are marked differences between the examples which can lead to confusion, especially where personal names are concerned. Here Domesday's *Aleuuoldestune*, the twelfth-century *Elwaldeston*, and *Ailwaldestone* and *Ailwaldeston* from the thirteenth century do not clarify whether the place-name means 'Aethelwald's settlement' or 'Aefwald's settlement'.

The castle at Elvaston was inherited in 1829 by Lord Petersham, the 5th Earl Harrington. He made no changes to the building, which had been entirely rebuilt twelve years earlier, but brought in William Barron, a gardener from Scotland, to improve the grounds. Within twenty years Barron (and his army of ninety gardeners) had turned what was little more than a few dozen assorted evergreens on a patch of wasteland into a series of spectacular tunnels, walkways and avenues, most of which we can still see today.

Within the parish are **Ambaston**, which was 'Eanbald's farm', and **Bellington Hill**, which is derived from 'Bella's farm'. **Harrington Villas** were built on land owned by the Earls of Harrington, the lords of the manor, while **Thurlston** was 'Thurulf's farm', and although the spelling of **Thurlstone Grange** has the extra letter its origins are identical.

Elvaston Hall is no longer occupied, but the gardens are still superbly maintained.

The remains of an early (unknown) construction in the grounds of Elvaston Hall.

Erewash, River

This river-name is listed as *Yrewis* in 1175, *Irewiz* in 1229 and *Irewys* in 1226. The second element here is the Old English *wisce* meaning 'stream', while the first element is *irre* from the same language, describing the watercourse as 'wandering or winding'.

Etherow

Listings such as *Ederhou* in 1226, *Ederou* in 1285 and *Edderowe* in 1290 are not much help in defining this river-name which is undoubtedly Old British or Celtic in origin. Normally the Welsh, Gaelic, Breton or Cornish tongues would give us some clues as to the meaning, but in this case the known forms are too late and too corrupted to enable us to offer any suggestions.

Etwall

With this name also represented locally by **Etwall Common**, **Etwall Hall** and **Etwall Lodge**, listings as *Etewelle* in Domesday and *Etewell* in 1185 show this is undoubtedly 'Eata's stream'.

A falconry reference from the French *en boucle*, meaning the hawk is tied by its leash to a ring, is the derivation of the **Hawk & Buckle Inn**.

Eyam

This unusual name is recorded as *Aiune* in Domesday and *Eyum* in 1236. This is the Old English *egum*, the dative plural of 'island' – eerily prophetic considering how the place isolated itself centuries later. There are other examples of similar names hereabouts, seen on today's maps as **Eyam Dale**, **Eyam Woodlands**, **Eyam Edge** and **Eyam Moor**.

Local names include **Fallcliff House**, which tells of 'the fallow steep slope'. **Grindleford Bridge** is something of a mystery for there is no sign of a ford ever having existed here. It may be that the suggested 'ford that was ground away' is the meaning here, in which case the eroded ford would now be lost. Hence if the definition is correct it can never be proven! **Toot Hill** is an accurate description of 'the flat-topped hill', **Leam** is another Saxon name telling us of the '(place at) the clearings', and **Old Twelve Meer's Mine** may have been an estimation as the pools were seasonal and only rarely were there exactly twelve of them.

This sundial on the wall of Eyam church shows much more than just the time. Designed by Mr Duffin, clerk to Mr Simpson of Stoke Hall, the work was done by William Shore, a local stonemason.

An eighth-century Celtic cross in Eyam churchyard. It is in remarkably good condition.

F

Fairfield

Listings from the thirteenth century differ only slightly from the modern form. This place is what it seems: the '(place at) the beautiful feld (cleared land)'. The intriguingly named **Cunning Dale** does not reveal tales of mystery from yesteryear, but hails from the Old Scandinavian *kunung dalr*, 'the king's valley'. **Nithen End** is a rather strange place-name, for it is derived from 'nothing end'. We can only assume this is suggesting that it was worthless ground, for if there was nothing there it surely would not have merited a name.

The 19th Hole is a pub name with an obvious golfing reference (for those who are not aware, this is the name given to the clubhouse where players relax with a post-round beverage and exchange golfing anecdotes).

Farley

The eleventh-century records of *Farleie* and *Farnleya* show this to be the Saxon *fearn-leah*, 'the woodland clearing covered with ferns'.

Fenny Bentley

Bentley is a name found throughout much of England. *Benedlege* in Domesday and *Fennibenetlegh* in 1272 clearly show this to be derived from the Old English *beonet-leah*, 'the clearing overgrown with bent grass'. The prefix refers to the region being 'marshy', which may well have been seasonal.

Ravenscliff may be derived from the 'bank where ravens are seen' or perhaps it is a personal name giving 'Hraefn's bank'. Whatever the origins of Ravenscliff, it seems the pre-Conquest locals were somewhat happier with their home than their descendants, for they coined some rather uncomplimentary minor names from the twelfth century onwards. What became **Sweat Doles** was actually intended to refer to 'the sweet dales', **Dirty Pasture** was inclined to become rather muddy, **Bastard Leys** is a common combination referring to its irregular shape, and **Broad Arse Piece** is from *brad-ears-pece*, 'broad-bottomed piece of land'.

Fernilee

This would seem to have the same origin as Farley but the listing of *Ferneleia* from 1108 shows that it is from the Saxon for 'the fenny or marshy woodland clearing'.

Local place-names include **Horwich End**, meaning 'the boundary elm', and **Shallcross Manor**, 'the cross to which a shackle or fetter is attached'. This is probably a reference to a pillory to which pilgrims were tied as a penance.

Findern

The records as *Findre* in 1086, *Findena* in 1188 and *Finderne* in 1204 show this to come from the Saxon *fin-renn*, 'the house for wood' – i.e. where supplies of wood were available, most likely for building. Locally the 'stream in a depression' today appears on maps as **Potlock**.

All Saints' Church at Findern was rebuilt in the 1860s, yet still contains parts of the original building. (Photo: Andy Savage)

Flagg

We have already noted that Derbyshire place-names were often influenced by the Scandinavian tongues, and in Flagg we find that influence again.

There is no known Old English word which we can attribute to the early forms of *Flagun* in 1086, *Flagge* in 1284 and *Flagh* in 1315. Middle English offers *flag*, 'a sod, turf', which is itself derived from a Scandinavian dialect word related to the Icelandic *flag*, describing 'a place where turf has been cut away'. Hence the most likely definition, given the information available, is that Flagg was a place where peat was cut for fuel, perhaps somewhere along **Flagg Lane** or on **Flagg Moor**, or even on the 'upper dale' which appears on today's maps as **Hubber Dale**.

The Bull in the Thorn at Flagg has an oak carving inside the pub depicting a bull entangled in a thorn bush. The carving dates from the fifteenth century, but we cannot tell if the carving was made to represent the name of the pub or vice versa. **The Plough Inn** is an example of the common agricultural references found in pub names; this particular name has been in existence since the sixteenth century.

Foolow

Around the beginning of the fourteenth century we find *La Foulowe* and *Fuwelowe*, which point to the Old English *fugol-hlaw*, the '(place at) the hill frequented by birds'.

Minor place-names in the region include **Duric Well**, named after former resident John Duric; **Slater's Mine**, referring to Ellis Slater, who was resident from at least 1683; and **Broster Field**, derived from 'browster', an occupational surname meaning 'brewer'.

Foremark

This is another example of the Old Scandinavian tongue, as seen from the listings as *Fornewerche* in Domesday and *Fornewerk* in 1242. Here the Old Scandinavian *fom-verk* gives 'the old fort', also used for the local names **Foremark Bottom**, **Foremark Hall** and **Foremark Park Farm**.

Foston

Doubtless the twelfth-century records of *Fostuna*, *Foxtuna* and *Fostun* point to its origins as 'Fot's tun or settlement'. The local **Foston Brook** is clearly named from the place, although it was undoubtedly known as something else in earlier times.

G

Glapwell

There are two schools of thought about the origins of this place-name. Some maintain it is from the Old English *glaeppa-wella*, 'buck-bean stream', but the majority believe it to be derived from a personal name, giving 'Glappa's stream'.

Local names include the highly unusual **Losk Corner**. Of uncertain origins, this may be derived from a British or Celtic word related to the Old Welsh *llosg*, Cornish *losk* and Breton *losc* meaning 'burning', indicating that fire was used to clear the area for building and/or agriculture.

Glossop

Luckily we have a number of recorded names here, as *Glosop* in 1086, *Glotsop* in 1219, *Glossope* in 1245 and *Gloshop* in 1290, otherwise we would have had some difficulty in finding the personal name giving 'Glott's hop, or valley'. Something similar is still seen on today's maps in **Glossop Dale**.

The Young Vanish public house at Glapwell marks the exploits of a famous racehorse.

Knob Fields road sign at Gresley.

Locally we find **Padfield**, which is of Saxon origin meaning 'Padda's open land', and **Hobroyd**, which comes from 'goblin clearing'. **Whitfield House** describes the area as the 'white or dry open land'. Early records do not make clear the exact origins of **Simmondley**; it may be either Old English 'Sigemund's clearing' or Old Scandinavian 'Sigmundr's clearing'.

That the region was heavily reliant on sheep farming is seen in pub names such as **The Drovers Arms**; for such men the inn was a welcome port of call on long and tiring journeys driving sheep to market. Among the many 'welcoming' pub names is the **Friendship Inn**, while **The Sparrows** tells of the delicacy known as sparrow pie or pudding, which was considered to make the diner sharp-witted. 'Advertising' signs include the **Grapes Inn**, which may have been displayed at an ale stake, possibly in the form of an oak tree – hence the **Old Oak**.

Gresley

I make no apologies for listing **Church Gresley** and **Castle Gresley** under the same heading, for in addition to sharing the same name they are also next-door neighbours. Indeed, there is reason to believe that both started life as one settlement, which split into two as the population grew from the original 'grove clearing'. The two additions both have obvious origins, although it should be noted that the 'Castle' was a hillfort and not the stone-built battlements which immediately spring to mind.

Griffe

The only record available to us dates from 1286 as *Grif*. This is most probably derived from the Old Norse *gryfia* and means 'a hollow or pit', the purpose of which is unknown.

Grindlow

Early records of this name are hardly required to define a name which is quite clearly a reference to the '(place at) the green hill or burial-mound'. Minor names locally are much more interesting, such as **Silence Mine**, a name created merely on the whim of the owner. This cannot be said of the name derived from the Saxon *saelig-dael*, meaning 'happy, prosperous dale', a reference to the fine returns given by high-quality agricultural land. I doubt if those who coined the name would recognise it on today's maps as **Silly Dale**.

H

Hackenthorpe

Listed as *Hakenthorp* in 1327 and *Hakunthorpe* in 1423, this name comes from the Scandinavian occupation of Derbyshire. This is 'Hacun's thorp, or outlying settlement'. The personal name Hacun is from Old Danish, and is related to the Old Swedish and Old Norse Hakon.

Haddon

There is no Haddon as such, but Nether Haddon and Over Haddon both incorporate the Old English *haeth-dun*, 'the heather-covered hill'.

Nether Haddon, listed as *Hadune* in Domesday and *Netherhaddon* in 1276, is 'the lower place at the heather-covered hill'. Over Haddon, *Hadun* in Domesday, *Uverehaddon* in 1206, *Ufrehedon* and *Ouerhaddon* in 1230, is 'the higher place at the heather-covered hill'. Nether Haddon has three local places with the same origins, **Haddon Fields**, **Haddon Hall** and **Haddon Park**, while Over Haddon has **Haddon Grove**.

Near Nether Haddon lies **Bouns Corner**, which is named after Richard Bown, a resident here in 1459, and **Housley Wood**, which recalls William Housley, who was here in 1854. Over Haddon's local names include **Blore's Barn Farm**, which was the property of Jonathan Blore in 1846.

Hadfield

Recorded as *Hetfelt* in Domesday and *Haddefeld* in 1185, this place-name comes from the Saxon *haeth-feld*, 'the heather-covered clearing'.

The Masons Arms may seem to be named after the Company of Masons, who cut stone for building purposes, especially as their arms granted in 1473 appear on the sign, but the name is more likely to refer to a meeting-place of the Freemasons.

The Palatine tells us it stands on land once owned by the Earl Palatine, which refers not to Derbyshire but Cheshire. The Earl Palatine had jurisdiction over an area which would normally belong to the monarch. The word comes from the Latin meaning 'pertaining to the palace', and is the basis for the Palatine Hill in Rome which was the site of the palace of the early Roman emperors.

Hallam

There are two Hallams in Derbyshire, the name being derived from the dative plural of the Saxon *halh*, 'nook, remote valley'. **Kirk Hallam** – *Burhhalum* in 1006, *Halum* in 1086 and *Kirkehalum* in 1242 – is the '(place at) the *halh* with a church'; **West Hallam** – *Buchhalum* in 1006, *Halum* in 1086 and *Westhalum* in 1230, is 'place at the *halh* to the west'.

Kirk Hallam has an inn called the **Cat & Fiddle**. Various explanations have been offered for the origins of this name, including the suggestion that it is derived from Catherine de Fidele, wife of Russia's Peter the Great, but the real origin is the obvious one, the children's rhyme which begins 'Hey Diddle Diddle, the cat and the fiddle.' Interestingly the pub name is known to have existed earlier than the rhyme's first appearance in print in the sixteenth century, over two centuries before Catherine's birth.

West Hallam has a **Punchbowl Inn**, a name which is intended to lure passers-by to sample the fare.

Handley

Although the only early record we can find is as *Henlege* in Domesday, there can be no doubt this is Saxon *hea-leah*, the '(place at) the high woodland clearing'. While Domesday's forms are not to be trusted, **Mid Handley** ('the middle high *leah*'), **Nether Handley** ('the lower high *leah*'), and **West Handley** ('the high *leah* to the west') have enough records available to prove the Saxon origins.

Hardstoft

Another place-name of Old Scandinavian origins, as seen by the records of *Hertestaf* in Domesday and *Hertistoft* in 1257, this is 'Heort's toft (homestead)'.

Hardwick

From the Old English *heorde-wic*, meaning 'herd farm', the place is almost totally within the estate of Hardwick Hall, once one of the most splendid buildings in the county and still a tremendous sight for the thousands of tourists who visit every year.

Harthill

This is 'the place at the hill frequented by stags'. Derived from Old English, it is recorded as *Hortil* in Domesday and *Herthil* in 1176. The same name is recorded locally as **Harthill Moor Farm**, **Harthill Moor Wood** and **Harthill Hall Farm**.

Nearby is **Hermit's Cave**, a name which needs no explanation, but it is worth mentioning the figure of Christ on the cross cut from the solid rock face, its worn appearance giving a guide as to how long ago it was worked.

Hartington

Of almost identical origins to Harthill, this is derived from the slightly different Saxon *heorta-dun*, the '(place at) the stag's hill'. It is recorded as *Hortedun* in Domesday, *Hertendon* in 1200 and *Hertindon* in 1251, and local names of identical origins include **Hartington Dale**, **Hartington Hall**, **Hartington Mill** and **Hartingtonmoor Farm**.

One local name is seen several times, as **Goyt's Bridge**, **Goyt's Clough**, **Goyt's Moss**, **Goyt's Lane** and **Goytshead Farm**, and is itself derived from a river-name which has survived from the pre-Roman British or Celtic language. Recorded as *Guit*, *Gwid*, *Gwit* and as the modern form in the thirteenth century, this is clearly related to the Welsh *gwyth*, meaning 'channel or conduit'.

Other minor names here are many and varied. **Cronkston Grange** is named from 'Crannuc's hill', the suffix which is seemingly *-tun* being a corruption of *-dun*. **Crowdecote** is derived from 'Cruda's cottage'. **Dowel** is named from the 'Dove spring', a small tributary of the main river. **High Wheeldon** originates in the 'hill with a stone circle', while **Hurdlow Town** tells of 'the treasure mound' (where the 'treasure' refers to anything worth having!). 'Cardel's enclosure' is today recalled in the lane which once led there, **Cardlemere Lane**, **The Frith** was 'the hunting forest', while **Harley**, 'a grey clearing', refers to an outcrop of limestone here. **Fern House** remembers fifteenth-century landowner Richard Ferne, **Booth** is derived from 'the herdsman's shed', **Pilsbury** was once 'Pil's fortified place', and **Ludwell** had a particularly 'loud spring' for its water supply.

Chrome Hill comes from the Old English *crumb*, meaning 'crooked, twisted, bent'; **Clemonseats Plantation** stands on land where 'Clement's houses' once stood; **Custard Field** is 'the apple field'; **Glutton** is a nickname from the Middle English *gloton*, suggesting 'wasted' or 'misused' land; **The Whim** was 'a machine to draw ore powered by horses'; **Plex Farm** tells us this was specifically 'small plots of land where hops grow'; and **Jericho** is one of the sarcastic names given to the furthest corner of a parish.

Hartshorne

This is another place-name with a similar meaning to Harthill and Hartington. Recorded as *Heorteshorne* in Domesday and *Herteshorn* in 1196, this is the '(place at) the stag's headland'. Local names include the quite descriptive **Short Hazels**, indicating that the trees had been pollarded. In 1741 one Nathaniel Moxon was in residence on or near **Moxon's Hill**.

The **Admiral Rodney** remembers the exploits of George Brydges, Lord Rodney (*c.* 1718–92), notably against the French at the Battle of Saintes in 1782. This was a major turning-point in Anglo-French relations which were at a very low ebb during the American Revolution.

In recent years **The Snooty Fox** has become a popular name, for no apparent reason other than it suggests a sense of style, is an obvious 'pub' name and allows sign painters a fair amount of artistic licence.

Hasland

Listed as *Haselund* in 1200, and *Heselund* and *Haseland* in 1276, this place-name is derived from the Old Scandinavian *heali-lundr*, the '(place at) the hazel grove'.

One local name which is rather unusual, although by no means unique, is **Philadelphia**, which has appeared on maps since at least 1840. However, despite being a relatively recent name there are no clues as to why the US place-name has been adopted by a small region of Derbyshire, for nothing has ever been found connecting any resident of Hasland with the City of Brotherly Love. Yet, as with all such transfers from afar, the place is on the border with the neighbouring parish, suggesting a 'far-flung' place. We know that these far corners of the parishes were often named after distant cities of the world, but we are rarely able to discover why the specific name was chosen. **Corbriggs** is much simpler, being easily seen as the '(place at) the cold bridge'.

Hassop

Listed as *Hetesope* in Domesday, *Hashop* in 1229 and *Hatsope* in 1236, this name is of Old English derivation as 'Haett's hop'. The Saxon *hop* is used specifically to describe 'dry land in a fen or marsh'.

Minor place-names in the area include **Back Dale Wood**, the '(place at) the valley beneath the ridge', and **White Coe Mine**, which is self-explanatory when we know that a coe was a small building where miners dress and store the ore.

Hathersage

This is an Old English or Saxon place-name, recorded as *Hereseige*, *Haueresheg*, *Haureshegg*, *Havershech* and *Hathersegge* in the two hundred years following the Domesday survey.

Hathersage lies in a valley close to a steep ridge known as Millstone Edge, and the name is made up of two elements, *haefer*, 'he-goat', and *ecg*, 'edge, steep ridge'.

Minor place-names here include **Granby Wood**, named after the Marquis of Granby, and **Fox House Inn**, which recalls local resident Nicholas Fox, who

An ornate road sign at Hathersage.

lived here in 1399. **Little John's Grave** is reputed to be the final resting-place of Robin Hood's right-hand man, in a plot measuring 14 feet in length outside the church. It once displayed a cap and bow said to belong to the giant.

Hatton

An Old English place-name, *haeth-tun*, 'the settlement on the heath', is recorded as *Hatune* in Domesday, and as *Hetton* and the modern form in 1230.

Hayfield

As mentioned previously, the Saxon *feld* may have identical origins to the modern 'field', but it cannot really be considered to be the same thing. The modern version is an enclosed area bordered by a wall, fence or hedgerow and used for agricultural purposes, be it crops or livestock. In contrast, the Saxon *feld* was not necessarily enclosed, at least not on all sides. It would have been used for growing crops or for grazing livestock under the watchful eye of the shepherd or herdsman.

Phoside Farm comes from the Old English *fag side*, the '(place at) the multi-coloured hill slope', referring to the soil colour. **Abbots Chair** refers to a boundary stone marking land held by the Abbot of Basingwerk. **Higginbottom** recalls the family of George Higginbotham of Swallowhouses who lived here from at least 1714. The area known as **Knarrs** is derived from *cnearr*, meaning 'rugged rock', and **Nab Brow** is 'the pointed outcrop of rock'.

Hazlebadge

Listed as *Heselebec* in Domesday and *Haselbech* in 1252, this is an Old English name meaning the '(place at) the hazel valley'. Local people who have left their names in the landscape include William Hartle, recorded here in 1658, seen in **Hartle Dale**; Thomas Hill, resident from at least 1809, remembered by **Hillrake Mine**; and the family of John and Thomas Jennings, who were here by 1847 and gave their name to **Jenning's Dale**.

Hazlewood

There is only one early record of note, as *Haselwode* in 1327, which merely confirms our initial thoughts that this is obviously a settlement at the 'hazel wood'.

Hazlewood was home to E.M. Hull, a lady who wrote the books *The Sheik* and *Son of the Sheik*, the film versions of which gave Rudolph Valentino the screen role for which he will always be remembered.

Initially found in a sixteenth-century story, **Puss in Boots** remains a popular pantomime character today and the feline who masterminds the eventual success of his master is the inspiration behind the pub name.

Heage (or High Edge)

Both names are recorded recently enough to be considered contemporary, and the former is clearly a shortened form of the latter. Recorded as *Hayheg* in 1251, *Heghegge* in 1330, *Heege* in 1471, and *Heegge* in 1485, this comes from the Old English *hea-ecg*, '(place at) the high edge or ridge'. The name is also found in **The Heage Tavern**.

A record of the community's daily life is found in the name of **The Tollgate**, the origins of which are obvious although it is likely that the public house merely stands on or near the site of the original toll-gate. **Nodinhill** was the home of Mary Nodyn by 1673, while **Starvehimvalley Farm** is an uncomplimentary name for an unproductive area of land. **Ambergate** takes its name from the river (*see* Amber), and a former toll-gate on the Matlock road.

Heanor

This is listed as *Hainoure* in Domesday and *Henovre* in 1236, and the meaning is fundamentally the same as that of Heage. Here the name is derived from the Old English (*aet*) *heann-ofre*, '(at) the high edge'.

The Butchers Company was granted arms in 1540 and the inns frequented by its members or run by someone who previously worked in the trade often took the name of the **Butchers Arms**. Innkeepers were quick to take advantage of potential trade in the naming of the **Market Hotel**.

Heanor's street names, as we would expect, reflect the history of the place, with a large number including the names of trees. Examples include **Lilac Grove**, **Maple Gardens**, **Orchard Rise** and the rustic-sounding **Leafy Lane**. Most places which adopt such names use them together on housing estates for some degree of continuity. Heanor, however, has utilised them all over the town.

The Derby Arms at Heanor.

Bircumshaw Road is named after one Isaac Bircumshaw, who was not only a tailor but also a purveyor of coal. The road was formerly known as **Back Lane**, for obvious reasons. **Ella Bank Road** recalls one of the daughters of John Holbrook, who was surveyor to Heanor Urban District Council.

One of Heanor's oldest street-names is **Burnthouse Road**, which appears on a map dating from 1792. It is said to derive its name from the burning down of a thatched cottage which stood near the junction with Derby Road. Previously the west end of the road had been known by what would now be considered a derogatory term. Tradition says this remembers a freed slave who lived here around 1840, but it may equally have been descriptive of the blackened faces of coalminers as they returned home from work to their purpose-built cottages.

Heath

This is from the Saxon *haeth*, recorded as *Heth* in the thirteenth century, and the settlement was located exactly where it says it was!

The **Elm Tree Inn** is another example of the ale stake origins discussed in the introduction. **Owlcotes** may seem to have the obvious origin of 'owl cottages', but the true definition is 'the old cottages', the corruption coming about through the regional pronunciation. Another 'old' name found here is **Old Peverel Road**, an indirect reference to the track to Bolsover Castle which was held by William Peveril. **Lound** is a Saxon name derived from 'grove, small wood', while 'the guild house ford' is certainly the origin of **Gildaforge Bridge** and yet no trace (either written or archaeological) has ever been found of any guild house here.

Heathcote

This is another simple and somewhat obvious place-name. Derived from the Saxon 'the cottage on the heath', it is listed as *Hedcote* in Domesday and *Hethcote* in the thirteenth century.

Higham

A place-name found in several places across England, usually with a second unique element. However, the Derbyshire version has never enjoyed the luxury of a distinctive addition, being listed simply as *Heyham* in 1284 and *Hegham* in 1330. The name comes from the Old English *heah-ham*, 'the high homestead'.

Highlow

What seems to be a fine example of an oxymoron proves to be quite the reverse when we examine the name in its original version. Listed as *Heghlawe*,

Heyelawe and *Heelowe* in the thirteenth century, the name is derived from the Saxon *heah-hlaw*, the '(place at) the high hill'.

Nearby we find **Dunge Wood**, 'well-manured land'; *Nickley*, 'Nick's meadow-land', with the second element coming from the Saxon *laes*; **The Oalers**, from the Old English alor, 'the alder trees'; and **Till Field**, a short form of Matilda, a lady about whom nothing is known.

Hilton

Records as *Hiltune, Hilton, Helton* and *Hulton* only serve to confirm this name has changed little since the Saxons built their *hyll-tun*, 'the settlement on a hill'.

At Hilton is **Wakelyn Old Hall**, the manor house of the Wakelyn family, where Mary, Queen of Scots is said to have stayed en route to Tutbury Castle. Later becoming an inn called the Bulls Head, it has been a private residence since the late nineteenth century.

Higham village cross.

Hipper, River

This is not a major river today and is unlikely to have been of any great importance in past millennia. The only records we have are as *Hypir* in 1276 and *Hipere* in 1350, which are not as helpful as we would hope. The only plausible origin offered suggests this may originate from a word derived from Saxon *hyper*, meaning 'osier'. Hence this may well be *hyper-ea* or *hyper-broc*, giving 'osier water' and 'osier stream' respectively.

Hognaston

A somewhat unusual name, this has yet to be conclusively defined. Early listings as *Ochenauestun* in Domesday and *Hokenaston* in 1241 show it has nothing whatsoever to do with 'hogs'. One possible solution is the Old English second element *aefesn* following a personal name, although such a combination would be highly unusual. However, as this is the only potential origin offered so far, we shall have to settle for 'Hocca's pasturage' at this time.

Holbrook

This is the name not only of the place but, predictably, of the local stream. Listed as *Holebroc* in 1086 and (*aqua de*) *Holebrok* in 1280, this is a Saxon name literally meaning 'hollow brook', understood as 'the brook running in a deep ravine'.

Hollington

The modern form contains the element *-ing-* which would normally indicate a preceding personal name, yet records such as *Holisurde* and *Holinwrth* show this is not the case. The true origin is the Old English meaning, the '(place at) the holly enclosure'.

Holme

Two places in Derbyshire share this name, one near Bakewell (*Holun* in 1086, *Hulm* in 1278 and *Holm by Bauquell*), the other near Brampton (*Holun* in 1086, *Hulme* in 1258, and *Hulm*). Both are derived from the Old Scandinavian *holmr*, meaning 'island', referring to dry land in a marsh.

Holmesfield

Despite the similarities with Holme, the origins here are quite different for this is of Saxon derivation. Recorded as *Holmesfelt* in Domesday and *Holmesfeld* in

1160, this is 'the *feld* (cleared land) belonging to Holme'. The Holme in question is that near Brampton, which lies only a few miles away.

Instantly recognisable as it can only be a pub name, **The George & Dragon** is a statement of national pride in the feats of England's patron saint, St George. **The Horns Inn** probably comes from the sounding of the post-horn which warned of the imminent arrival of the stage-coach. Horns were also used by huntsmen, and by draymen to give the landlord the chance to open his cellars ready for the delivery.

Local names include **Cartledge**, which is 'the slow stream in rough common land'; **Smeekley Wood**, its name reflecting its position on 'the smooth steep slope'; and **Horsleygate**, which was held by Adam de Horseley around 1388. From the Old Norse *birki*, **Birks** is 'the place overgrown with birch trees', while **Shillito Wood** was held by Jonathan Shillito in 1857.

Hoon

Early records as *Hougen*, *Howyn*, *Howene*, *Howen* and *Hawen* as well as the modern form can only originate from the Old Scandinavian *haugum*, the dative plural of *haugr*, meaning 'hill or mound'.

Hope

Usually found as the second element of a place-name, this is derived from the Old English *hop*, meaning 'valley'.

The minor names here show a little more imagination. **The Halsteads** is the site of a Roman camp and is derived from the Old English meaning 'nook of enclosed pasture'. **King's Haigh**, meaning 'king's enclosure', reflects the fact that Hope was a royal manor. **Twitchill Farm** lies alongside an ancient footpath leading over nearby Win Hill, which gives the farm its name from 'a narrow footpath'. **Dome Ridings** is a field-name coming from 'dam clearing'. The unusually named **Salto Furlong** is now only a field-name but originally referred to a 'salty spring or stream'. **Shirly Yard** is another field-name recalling Randolph Schirlegh who lived here in 1463, while another resident Robert Wodereue, recorded here in 1306, gave his name to **Woodroofe Pingle**.

It was common practice in the early days of Christianity for the local clergy to tour the parish boundaries at least once a year, stopping at specific points in order to bless the land, hoping thereby to deter evil spirits and encourage bumper crops. Yet to date nobody has any idea why the boundary stones marking this part of Hope's boundary are called **Madwoman's Stones**.

Minor names around the region of **Hope Woodlands** have various derivations. **Toadhole Cote** is a Saxon name meaning '(place at) the fox-earth', while **Marebottom Farm** comes from the same tongue giving 'pond in the valley'. Personal names are seen in **Gillethey Farm**, or 'Gillot's enclosure', and **Cocksbridge**, after John Cock, resident in 1626. **Wooler Knoll** means 'wolves' hill', perhaps recalling an individual's nickname. **Lockerbrook Farm** and **Lockerbrook Coppice** recall a very early farming settlement as 'the brook by an enclosure'. **Crook Hill** is from a Celtic or Old British word related to the Old Welsh *cruc*, meaning 'hill', and hence the modern form literally means 'hill hill'.

Hopton

Listed as *Opetune* in Domesday and *Hopton* in 1251, this place has the same origins as Hope, found here with an additional element giving 'the settlement in the valley'.

Hopwell

Once again, as with Hope and Hopton, the Saxon *hop* is seen here, this time producing the 'stream in a valley'. It is recorded as *Opeuuelle* in 1086, *Hopewell* in 1197 and in the modern form as early as 1242.

Horsley

Horselei in 1086 and *Horselee* in 1212 would seem to suggest an equine origin, which is indeed the case. From the Old English *horsa-leah*, this is the '(place at) the pasture for horses'. Perhaps landowner William Abbot, who held **Abbot's Rough** by 1773, allowed his horses to graze land that was unsuitable for crops. One local family is remembered by the name **Dobholes**: Ann Dob is the earliest known individual, resident here by 1770.

Horston

Listed as *Harestan* in 1205, this place-name comes from the Old English *hara-stan*, meaning literally 'the grey stone'. This probably indicates a boundary stone.

Hough

The Old English *hoh*, seen as *Hogh* in Domesday and *Hogh* in 1285, is the origin here, meaning the '(place at) the spur of the hill'.

Houghton

There are two such-named places in Derbyshire, both containing the same element found in Hough. New Houghton is recorded as *Holtune* in 1086,

Hochtone in 1280 and *Hoghton* in 1289. Here the Old English *hoh-tun* refers to the '(new) settlement on a spur of the hill'. Stoney Houghton has the same origins, with the addition referring to 'stony ground'.

Hucklow

Recorded as *Hochelai* in Domesday, *Parva Hokelawe* in 1253, *Hukelowe* in 1265 and *Magna Huckelowe* in 1301, the second element comes from the Old English *hlaw*, giving 'Hucca's mound or hill'. Here **Duce Farm** (and **Duce Hole**) recall ownership by the Douce family from at least 1630.

Hulland

From the Old English *hoh-land*, found as *Hoilant* in 1086, *Holond* in 1249 and *Holand* in 1262, this place-name tells of 'the land on or near a spur of the hill'.

Hungry Bentley

The name Bentley is quite common and is derived from the Old English *beonet-leah*, 'clearing overgrown with bent grass'. The addition is first seen in the mid-fifteenth century and is thought to be a reference to poor-quality soil requiring a great deal of fertiliser.

Hurdlow

An interesting name, this is recorded as *Hordlawe* in 1244 and *Hardlowe* in 1251. The Old English *hord-hlaw* is the basis for Hurdlow, as the '(place at) the treasure mound'. The first element is easily seen as being related to the modern 'hoard'.

I

Ible

Listed as *Ibeholon* in Domesday and *Ibole* in 1288, the modern form is a contraction of the Old English *Ibban holu*, 'Ibba's hollow or valley'. The name is also found in **Ible Wood**.

Idridgehay

The second element comes from the Old English or Saxon *haeg*, meaning 'enclosure'. There can be no doubt about the personal name, seen in records as *Edtichesei* in 1230, *Iriggehay* in 1252 and *Eddricheshey* and *Iddurshey* in 1484: this is 'Eadric's enclosure'.

Less certain is the origin of **Wallstone Farm**, which is probably 'Walh's farm' or less likely the 'farm of the serf'. What is certain is that it does not refer to any dry-stone wall(s) surrounding the farm, for place-names were used principally to differentiate places, and such walls are very common throughout Derbyshire. Hence to suggest that the reference is to the farm walls is illogical and can be instantly discounted even before consulting early records.

Ilkeston

There are plenty of early forms for us to study here, including *Tilchestune* in 1086, *Elchesdona* in 1155, *Hilkesdon* in 1236, *Ilkesdon* in 1242, *Elkesdon* in 1252 and *Ilkesdon* at the end of the thirteenth century. These records not only help to define the meaning, but also enable us to see something of the name's evolution. From the Old English personal name, this is 'Ealac's hill', with the second element coming from the Saxon *dun*, used in the sense 'down'.

As with all public houses so named, the **Commercial Inn** was specifically tailored to suit the needs of commercial travellers and was named to advertise that fact to prospective clients. **The Concorde** records the flight of the supersonic airliner, and has much more recent beginnings. The **Gallows Inn** is predictably located near the site of a former gallows. The **Dewdrop Inn** is said to have taken its name from the motto of the Distiller's Company, itself a quote from the 'Song of Moses' in Deuteronomy 32:2, 'My speech shall distil as the dew.' This somewhat contrived definition can be discarded in favour of the more obvious invitation to 'do drop in'. Named after the 1919 novel by

The sign of the Mallard public house, on the outskirts of Ilkeston.

Somerset Maugham, the **Moon & Sixpence** has the added bonus of being a simple design to depict on the sign.

Ilkeston was first granted a charter for a market and street fair in 1252 and its street names reflect the long history of the town. **Cantelupe Road** is named after the Lords of Ilkeston, the first of whom was Nicholas de Cantilupe in 1261. Built on land owned by the Stanton Iron Works, **Glandon Road** is named after the company's quarry in Northamptonshire. **Graham Street** recalls the exemplary military career of Sir Gerald Graham (1831–99), who served his country in the Crimea, Egypt, China and Sudan. The role played by Major-General Sir Henry Havelock in the Sepoy Mutiny of 1857 is celebrated in both **Havelock Street** and the **General Havelock Inn**.

At the end of the nineteenth century a family of brickmakers gave their name to **Horridge Street**. **Keppel Court** is named after the British naval officer Viscount Augustus Keppel (1725–86). **Muskham Avenue** recalls the family name of the lords of the manor of Ilkeston from the twelfth century, when it was bestowed on the Muskham family by Gilbert de Gand, nephew of William the Conqueror. **Pedley Street** is named after John Pedley, a nineteenth-century local landowner, and **Wakefield Place** recalls former resident, shopkeeper and baker John Wakefield.

A map of the area also includes minor place-names such as **Barker's Lock**, recalling landowner Richard Barker who was here in 1691. In the same year John Dodson had ties with **Dodson House**. **Skeavington's Farm** was run by Nicholas Skevington in 1593, **Stenson's Lock** remembers Robert Stenson who was in residence by 1696, and John Straw who lived here in 1670 is commemorated by **Straw's Bridge**.

Ingleby

As noted previously in this book, Derbyshire was occupied in part by the Scandinavian peoples at various times during the Anglo-Saxon era. It should not be thought, however, that it was a precise demarcation and certainly there were areas where Scandinavians lived in Saxon territory and vice versa. The origins of Ingleby provide us with evidence of just such an area. Listed as *Englaby* in 1009, *Englebi* in 1086 and *Engleby* in 1228, the name comes from the Old Scandinavian *Englabyr*, 'the village of the English'.

John Thompson pub sign.

Inkersall

This is more often found as West Inkersall, although the addition 'West' is now really superfluous. It is recorded as *Hinkershil* in 1242, *Hinckreshill* in 1264 and *Hinkershill* in 1290. Obviously the initial H has been lost over the years, but it points to the possible origin as Old English *higna-aecer*, the '(place at) the cleared land of the monks'. Alternatively it might refer to the '(place at) the cleared land of the Hiwan', a Saxon tribe.

Ireton

There are no fewer than three Iretons in Derbyshire: **Kirk Ireton**, **Little Ireton** and **Ireton Wood**. These places are listed as *Hiretune* and *Iretune* in Domesday, with a single reference to *Little Ireton* in 1315. Ireton is derived from the Old English for 'the tun (settlement) of the Irish'. To differentiate between the three the additions 'with a church', 'smaller' and 'in the wood' respectively were tacked on to the initial element.

Ivonbrook

Listed as *Winbroc* in Domesday, *Ivelbrok* in 1269 and *Yuenbroc* at the end of the thirteenth century, this name is derived from the Old English for 'Ifa's brook'.

    Wigleymeadow Farm is named after a former owner, John Wigley, who lived here from around 1649.

K

Kedleston

Found in Domesday as *Chetelestune* and in a record dating from 1206 as *Ketleston*, this was 'Ketel's tun or settlement'. The origins of **Vicar Wood** are not what they seem but a reference to 'bee-keeper wood', while **Moodersley** was 'Mothir's pasture' in pre-Conquest times.

Kedleston Hall is described by Pevsner as 'the most splendid Georgian house of Derbyshire', and it was the home of the most powerful family in Kedleston, at least since the Norman Conquest. For 800 years the Curzons dominated this place, culminating in the achievements of George Nathaniel Curzon, Marquess of Kedleston (1859–1925), who was appointed Viceroy of India and Foreign Secretary, and was within touching distance of becoming Prime Minister in 1923, until George V opted instead for Stanley Baldwin.

Kidsley

Recorded as *Kidesleage* in 1009, *Chiteslei* in 1086, *Kideslea* in 1176 and *Kidesleia* in 1200, the second element is derived from the Saxon *leah*, giving the '(place at) Cyddi's woodland clearing'.

Kilbourne

From the Old English *cylenburna*, meaning the '(place at) the stream by a kiln', it occurs in records as *Killebrun* in 1200, and *Killeburn* and *Kileburn* in 1236.

Killamarsh

Recorded as *Chinewoldemaresc* in Domesday and *Kinewaldesmers* in 1249, this is another place-name of Saxon origin meaning 'Cynewald's marsh'.

In the days when the horse was king of the road the sign of the **Blacksmiths Arms** told travellers that the village smithy was available to care for their horses while they filled their stomachs and quenched their thirst. The **Bull & Badger** is an odd combination, probably the result of the amalgamation of two separate inns which were either owned by the same person or joined forces because of insufficient custom.

Kinder

Recorded as *Chendre* in Domesday and *Kynder* in 1285, there seems little doubt this place-name recalls that of the highest point in the Peak District, Kinder Scout, at 2,088 feet. As with many river-names and hill-names the origins here are Old British or Celtic, the tongue spoken by the inhabitants of England in the pre-Roman era, which is known largely through its close resemblance to modern Welsh, Gaelic, Cornish and Breton.

The probable origin of Kinder Scout is *Cunetio-briga* (the Welsh form would be *Cynwydfre*), the second element referring simply to a 'hill'. The first element is an unknown word, but is related to Old Norse *skuti*, 'overhanging rock'. The **River Kinder** is another example of a river-name taking that of the settlement, rather than retaining its original name.

Kirk Ireton

Ireton, or Kirk Ireton, appears as *Hiretune* and *Iretune* in Domesday, and is derived from the Old English for 'the tun (settlement) of the Irish'. The additional Kirk, for the church, distinguishes it from other Iretons elsewhere in the county.

Kirk Langley

This name is derived from the Saxon *lang-leah*, the '(place at) the long woodland clearing'. Kirk Langley, recorded as *Chirchelongeley* in 1273, has the addition to show the place has a church. **Meynell Langley**'s distinctive addition, first recorded in 1284, shows that this was held by one Robertus de Maisnell. This family name is derived from one of the places named Mesnils in France. The Old French *mesnil*, related to the Latin *monsionile*, simply means 'village'. There is also a **Langley Green** and a **Langley Hall**, both with obvious meanings.

Kniveton

This is an interesting place-name, recorded as *Cheniuetun* in Domesday and *Kniueton* in 1169. The origin here is the Old English *cneo-tun*, literally 'the settlement at a knee', referring to a bend in a road. There is also a **Kniveton Wood** which takes its name from the place.

To us a road bend may seem unimportant but we should remember that during the era in question there were very few roads and even fewer had any 'bends' in them. It is a popular misconception that the earliest road system in England was built by the Romans, but this is not strictly accurate. In truth the

Roman occupation saw tremendous improvements made to the existing road system, which consisted simply of worn dirt tracks that had themselves been marked out long before. The need to trade with other encampments meant that people had to be able to travel quickly and easily between hillforts and most of the tracks so produced ran more or less in straight lines, marked out by men with staves who left 'markers' along the way. One of the most common markers on the ancient trackways was a tumulus or barrow. One local place-name shows that one such existed here for **Wigber Low** began life as 'Wicga's barrow'.

L

Langley

There are three places in Derbyshire so named, all of them derived from the Saxon *lang-leah*, the '(place at) the long woodland clearing'. Langley near Heanor is found in Domesday as *Langeleie*. (*See also* Kirk Langley.)

Boundary post between the parishes of Langley and Brailsford on the A52.

Langwith

This place is usually known as Upper Langwith, although the distinction is now superfluous. It is recorded as *Langwath* in 1208. This early record shows the name to be derived from the Old Scandinavian *langa-vao*, 'the long ford', with later corruptions being influenced by the Old Scandinavian *vidr*, 'wood', and the Old English *worth*, 'enclosure'.

Lathkil

The only record of any note is as *Lathkell* in 1308. Yet this is of little help and the etymology of this place-name remains obscure.

Lea

It is unusual to find the Old English *leah* standing alone, as it is normally found as a second element. Yet the records of *Lede* in Domesday and *Lee* in 1326 show this cannot be anything else, hence this is the '(place at) the woodland clearing'.

The range of 'advertising' and 'welcoming' pub names increases every year in the modern era. While **The Jug & Glass Inn** may not have the most imaginative name, it does give the sign painter a simple image to portray and it is unmistakably the name of a public house.

Linton

As we only have early forms such as *Linton* in 942, *Linctune* in 1086 and *Linton* in 1242, it is difficult to state conclusively whether the first element here is the Old English *lin* or *lind*. The former would indicate a 'flax settlement', the latter a 'lime-tree settlement', possibly the trees which then dominated the edges of what is known as **Linton Heath**.

The Hollybush would have been a local landmark and an example of an ale stake. Now associated with Christmas, holly was used by the Romans for decorations during the Feast of Saturnalia, also celebrated in December. Saturn was the Roman god of agriculture and his feast began on the shortest day of the year, with seven days of riotous debauchery celebrating the new growing season. This was easily replaced by the Christian Christmas festival. Indeed, 25 December was chosen as Christ's nativity because of the existing festival.

Litchurch

Recorded as *Ludecerce* in Domesday, *Litlecherche* in 1197 and *Lutchurch* in 1212, this is of Old English derivation, and means 'place with a small church'.

Little Chester

Listed as *Cestre* in Domesday and *Chestre* in 1229, this place takes its name from the Saxon *ceastre*, 'a Roman station'. The addition distinguishes it from the larger and better known administrative centre of neighbouring Cheshire.

Littleover

Recorded in Domesday as *Ufre* and *Parva Ufre*, this is a name of Saxon origin meaning 'the little place at the slope or ridge'.

Litton

Recorded as *Litun* in 1086, *Litton* in 1273 and *Lutton* in 1302, the Old English origin here is *hlydan-tun*, meaning 'the tun (settlement) on a torrent'. Alternatively, the origin may be a proper name, as *Hlydan-tun*, giving 'the tun on the river Hlyde', although the meaning of this river-name is ostensibly the same. Local place-names of the same origin include **Litton Dale**, **Litton Edge**, **Litton Frith**, **Litton Mill**, **Litton Slack** and **Littonfields**.

Nearby **Hammerton Hill** is derived from the Saxon **hamol dun**, telling us this was known as 'the scarred hill'.

Locko

Recorded in the thirteenth century as *Lokhaye*, *Lochay* and *Lokhawe*, this place-name is derived from the Old English *loc-haga*, both elements meaning 'enclosure'.

Longdendale

Like Locko, this name also has a 'double' element. Listed as *Langedenedele* in 1086 and *Langedenedala* in 1158, this is the '(place at) the valley of Longden', with Longden itself also meaning 'the long valley'.

Longford

Recorded in 1197 as *Langeford*, this place-name, predictably, is derived from the '(place at) the long ford', also giving rise to **Longford Park** and **Longfordlane**. Originating from different sources, both with a personal name as the first element, are **Bupton**, the '(place at) Bubba's hill', and **Mammerton**, 'Melmor's farmstead', while **Papermill Cottage** reveals that paper was produced here, as documented as early as 1681.

It may come as a surprise to discover that until 4 May 1870 all English cheese was made in farms and homes across the land. The first English cheese factory was built at Longford in 1870, under the management of Cornelius Schermerhorn – whose name surely merits a street-name!

Longstone

This is actually two places, Great Longstone and Little Longstone. Early listings include *Langesdune* in Domesday, *Langsdune* in 1225 and *Langesdone* in 1258. It is located close to a lengthy ridge, which itself may have been called 'long', to which the Saxons added the explanatory *dun*, meaning 'hill, down'.

Local names of interest include **Blakedown Hollow**, 'the black valley'; **Five Penny**, thought to refer to the rent charged; **Flaggy Leah**, the 'clearing where flagstones abound'; **Scratter**, from the Old Norse *skratti*, 'poor (literally scratchy) land'; and **Brandy Bottle**, a field named for its shape.

Although of obvious meaning and derivation, other field-names which cannot be omitted are **Aniseed**, **Bland Pasture** and **Arse o'th Ley**. Although at first it may seem strange for a fairly imposing hill to take its name from the comparatively insignificant stream which flows down its flanks, this is the case with **Ranhill**, which is 'small stream' with the suffix actually a reference to the stream, and not the hill down which it flows.

Finally we come to what must be one of the most delightful names anywhere in the county of Derbyshire, perhaps in the whole country. Lead was once mined in the area known as **Cacklemackle**, which tells us that it produced only 'the poorest kind of lead-ore yielding only smitham'.

Loscoe

Derived from the Old Scandinavian *loftskogr*, as seen by the records of *Loscoew* in 1277 and *Laschowe* in 1401, this means the '(place at) the wood on a hill'.

Street-names in Loscoe are equally unusual. **Clayton Grove** recalls the farming family living at Ash Farm, while **Glue Lane** is a corruption of John Glew, a prominent local landowner and churchwarden for Codnor and Loscoe from 1642. **Flamstead Avenue** marks the unique achievements of John Flamsteed, who was appointed the first Astronomer Royal on 4 March 1675. His parents moved to Crowtrees in Denby following an outbreak of the plague in Derby and it was at Crowtrees that John was born in August 1646. **Leniscar Avenue** is named after the fictional name given to Loscoe by Mary Howitt in her book *My Uncle the Clock Maker*. The uncle in question was Francis Tantum, actually the brother of the author's mother-in-law. On the front of Loscoe Baptist Chapel can be seen the initials FT and the date 1722, which undoubtedly refers to Mr Tantum.

Furnace Lane, Loscoe.

Where we've been and where we're going, Lullington.

Ludwell

Domesday's listing as *Lodouuelle* is the only early example available, but it is enough to enable us to define this as the '(place at) the loud stream'.

Ludworth

Domesday's *Lodeuorde* and the twelfth-century record as *Ludewurda* show this place to be derived from the Old English for 'Luda's worth, or fortified enclosure', also seen in **Ludworth Intakes** and **Ludworth Moo**r.

Lullington

A picturesque village on the border with Staffordshire, this place is listed in Domesday as *Lullitune* and in the mid-thirteenth century as *Lullingtone*. It is derived from the Saxon *Lulla-inga-tun*, 'the settlement of the people or the followers of Lulla'.

M

Mackley

There are three early records of note here, *Makelai* in 1150, *Mackele* in 1210 and *Mackeleg* in 1252, but none of these enables us to be certain that this is 'Macca's forest'.

Mackworth

Records such as *Macheuorde* in Domesday and *Mackeworth* in 1211 show this place has the same personal name as Mackley, being 'Macca's fortified enclosure'.

Makeney

Once again this incorporates the same personal name seen in Mackley and Mackworth. The second element is from the Old English *-eg*, giving 'Macca's island, or dry land in marsh'. The place is recorded as *Machenie* in Domesday and *Makeneye* in 1236.

Mapperley

The only early record available is *Maperlie* in Domesday, but there can be no doubt this is the '(place at) the woodland clearing where maple trees grow'.

The **Old Black Horse** derives its name from heraldic sources, with the prefix telling us it pre-dated a nearby rival.

Mappleton

The sole record is Domesday's *Mapletune*, giving 'the settlement by the maple trees'. Interestingly the locals spell it 'Mapleton', and it will be interesting to see which form endures.

Markeaton

Listed as both *Marchetone* and *Merchetune* in 1086, *Marketon* in 1236 and *Markenton* in 1251, this name originates from the Saxon *mearcea-tun*, 'the settlement on the boundary river'. The name is also seen in the local names of **Markeaton Brook, Markeaton Hill, Markeaton Park** and **Markeaton Stones.** The area known as **The Roundabout** is not an early traffic junction, but a roughly circular region surrounded by trees – literally with trees 'round about'.

Marston Montgomery

Marston is a common place-name, often found with a distinctive addition as here. This place-name comes from the Old English *mersc-tun*, 'the settlement by a marsh'. The first record of the addition dates from 1350, although we do know this place was held by William de Mungumeri a century earlier. The family name derives from the town in Normandy.

Local names of similar origins include **Marston Woodhouse, Marston Lodge, Marstonbank Farm** and **Marstonpark. Clownholme** is, at least in part, derived from the pre-Roman tongue known as British (Celtic) and related to Welsh, Cornish and Breton. Here the river-name *colauno* which means simply 'river, water' gives 'the homestead at (the River) Cloun'. Less complicated to define is **Wadley**, from the Old English meaning 'Walda's clearing'.

Marston-upon-Dove

Identical to the previous entry, this is the 'settlement by a marsh', this time on the River Dove. Locally **Halfcroft** is a corruption of the original 'Api's croft', while **Moorend** was 'furlong of wasteland'.

Matlock

Listed as *Meslach* in Domesday, *Matlac* in 1196, *Mathlac* in 1233 and *Matloc* in 1204, this place-name is derived from the Old English *maethl-ac*, 'the oak tree where a moot (meeting) is held'. The name has also been taken for the local names of **Matlock Bank, Matlock Bath, Matlock Bridge, Matlock Cliff, Matlock Green, Matlock Mill, Matlock Moor** and **Matlock Wood Farm.**

The **Masson Cavern** is a popular tourist attraction which takes its name from the valley below, which is 'Maessa's valley'. On the hill opposite the **Heights of Abraham** (named after the storming of Quebec in 1759) is **Riber** or 'rye hill'. **Willersley** began life as 'Wilheard's woodland clearing'; **Handkerchief Piece** is a somewhat sarcastic description of 'a small piece of land'; **Popecarr** is 'Pope's clearing', named from a personal name and not the religious office; **Dimple** refers to a hollow in the land and is the name of an old mine; the clearing of **Fantom Hag** was once thought to be haunted; while the greatest misnomer in the county must be **Toilet Wood**, which should be 'toil at'!

The River Derwent at Matlock Bath.

Named after his victory at Waterloo and his subsequent political career, the **Duke of Wellington** is a popular pub name throughout the country. Fed by the thermal waters (discovered in 1698) of the spa town, the **Fishpond Hotel** stands across the main road from the pond itself, which contains many more coins than it does ornamental fish. The pond also contains a milestone which reads: 'Chatsworth 10 miles, Bakewell 10 miles, Manchester 45 miles.' The stone is actually under the surface of the water and is currently so covered in algae as to be barely noticeable.

Just downstream from Matlock Bath is the world's first convex weir. Before this all weirs were concave, and indeed the vast majority still are. In truth the radical design was due to an error on the part of the constructors, but two centuries later it is still doing the job as well as ever!

Mease, River

This tributary of the Tame is recorded as *Meys* in 1247 and is probably derived from the Saxon *meos*, meaning 'mossy'. Other early forms include *Meis*, *Mays* and *Mese*, all of which reflect Anglo-Norman influences, showing how the two languages were merging to evolve into Middle English. While it is difficult to see the Norman-French influence on Old English in general language, proper names often show how French pronunciation had an effect.

Meersbrook

Listed as *Merebroc* and *Meresbroch* in the mid-twelfth century, the name means 'boundary brook'. It marks the boundary between Yorkshire and Derbyshire.

Melbourne

Early records include *Mileburne* in Domesday and *Meleburn* in 1164, showing this to be the '(place at or with) a mill stream', the name being adopted by **The Melbourne Arms** and the **Melbourne Hotel**.

Peniston Lamb took the name Lord Melbourne for his new peerage, his son later becoming Prime Minister. The Australian city is named in his honour. The pool where a tench approaching double figures was landed as the author turned after photographing **Melbourne Hall** stands in 20 acres of nineteenth-century landscaping.

The importance of sheep farming to the area is indicated by the **Lamb Inn**, although there is a chance it may have heraldic connections too. **The Roebuck** is another animal name, this time referring to the male of the small species of spotted deer.

Local names of note include **The Wiggs**, which is derived from Old Norse *veggr*, 'wall, boulder'; **Gun Croft** is a reference to the Gun family who were certainly here before the first record in 1673; and **New York**, a boundary region which was given a 'far-flung' name as a comment on its distance from the main settlement.

Mellor

Recorded as *Melner* in 1330, this name comes from the Old British language spoken in pre-Roman times and is identical with Welsh *moelfre*, 'bare hill'. This place is on the slope of a prominent hill, and the name is also seen in **Mellor Hall** and **Mellor Moor**. The map shows a region known as **Birchenough**, although little remains of what was once 'the birch-covered corner of land'.

Mercaston

Examination of records between 1086 and 1297 reveals references to this place as *Merchenestune, Murkelistone, Murkamstone, Murcaston, Murcaneston* and *Murkanston*. Of these we can justifiably disregard Murkelistone and Murkamstone as erroneous. This leaves us with three Saxon elements in *myrce-east-tun*, 'the eastern settlement on the dark river'. There is a strong possibility that the first element is an old name for **Cutler Brook**, yet **Mercaston Brook** is certainly an example of a name created by back-formation. The original name was probably related to the earlier name Cutler Brook.

The church at Melbourne is dedicated to St Michael with St Mary. It has been described as a 'cathedral in miniature'.

The Manor House at Melbourne has changed much since the original building by the bishops of Carlisle in the twelfth century.

Staunton Harold reservoir near Melbourne.

Here at Mercaston is a very small place of worship with the extraordinary name of **Halter Devil Chapel**. Apparently one Francis Brown, a farmer with a liking for drink, drunkenly bragged that the thunderstorm raging outside would not prevent him from riding to Derby that very night even if he had to 'halter the Devil'. In the dark he found it impossible to halter his mount, especially after a flash of lightning revealed his horse had horns. Brown fainted, as the 'Devil' returned to munching grass and chewing the cud. After taking a vow of sobriety the farmer duly built the chapel in 1723.

Merril Sick, River

What this small river lacks in stature it more than makes up for with its strategic importance and its interesting name. A tributary of the Meden in Nottinghamshire, this stream has long marked the boundary between the two counties. It is no surprise to find this rather unusual name is derived from the Old English *(ge)maere-wella*, 'the boundary stream', to which *sic*, 'small stream', was added quite early. The fact that there are two suffixes with virtually identical meanings seems to suggest that both names were in local use.

Mickleover

Early records show this place as *Magna Oufre*, *Magna Uure* and *Magna Oura*, all of which indicate this is a Saxon name meaning 'the larger place at the slope or ridge' (*see* Littleover). Local names include many references to water, including **Watergo Lane**, 'the watercourse', and **Cawdy Hill**, 'hill with a cold stream'.

Middleton by Wirkworth

This is 'the middle tun or settlement'. Domesday's *Middeltune* and the late thirteenth-century listing of *Midelton juxta Wyrkesworth* show when this fairly common place-name acquired its unique suffix, the origins of which are discussed under Wirkworth.

Locally we find **Smerrill**, a desirable 'hill with good pasture' for the farmer to graze his livestock. **Kiln Plantation** may have later been used for growing a variety of crops, but originally it was connected with lead-mining, being the place where the ore was smelted. **Bateman's Tomb** is the place where Thomas Bateman, who died in 1861, was buried after he had specifically demanded that his remains be interred in unconsecrated ground. His wife was also buried here.

Stoney Middleton, recorded as *Middleton juxta Heyum* in 1283, is another 'middle settlement', this time on stony ground, while the names **Middleton Cross**, **Middleton Moor** and **Middleton Wood** are of obvious origin. **Barbers Croft** is named after John Barber, who held land here in 1652, **Capps Close**

refers to William Capps, who lived here in 1682, Samuel Frost gave his name to **Frost Acre** in the mid-nineteenth century, and **Three Roods** is derived from Saxon *preo-rod*, 'three clearings'.

Milford

Although the only early record is Domesday's somewhat inaccurate *Muleforde*, there can be no doubt this is the '(place at) the ford by a mill'. Today **The Mill House** pub keeps the memory alive. **Chevin House** was erected on land which gave it its name, meaning 'the ridge of land'; **Hopping Hill** was 'where wild hops grow'; 'Maca's well-watered land' is today known as **Makeney**; and **Swainsley Court** was erected on what was once 'Sveinn's woodland clearing'. Although it hardly needs a major investigation to find out its origins, **Depth o' Lumb** is surely one of the most 'English' of Derbyshire's place-names. The Saxon *lum* or *lumm* is a word found mainly in the northern counties of England to describe a 'pool'.

Milton

There are two Miltons in Derbyshire, both with quite different origins. Milton near Repton comes from the Old English *mylen-tun*, 'the settlement by or with a mill'. Milton near Chapel en le Frith is listed in Domesday as *Middeltune*, which shows that the modern form is a corruption and it should have become another Middleton, 'the middle settlement'.

The **Swan Inn** is an heraldic reference usually associated with either Edward III or Henry VIII, but it is unclear what the association with either of these monarchs is here.

Monsal

This unusual place-name is recorded as *Morleshal* and *Morneshale* in the early thirteenth century. The second element is undoubtedly Old English *halh*, 'nook of land', but without further examples the first part remains a mystery.

Monyash

This delightful place-name is listed as *Maneis*, *Moniasse* and *Moniasche* between the eleventh and thirteenth centuries, and originates from the '(place at) many ash trees'.

Minor place-names of note in Monyash include **Knotlow**, 'Cnotta's burial-mound', and **One Ash Grange**, the '(place at) one ash-tree', with Grange added from the fourteenth century. **Bagshaw Dale** recalls former resident Edmund

Bagshaw, who was here by 1670, while Pinfold was an 'enclosure for animals'. **The Whim** refers to 'a machine used to draw ore, worked by horses'.

Morley

The record from 1002 as *Morlege* indicates this is derived from the Saxon for the '(place at) the woodland clearing by a moor or fenland'. Local names of identical origin include **Morley Hall**, **Morley Hayes**, **Morley Lime** and **Morleymoor**.

Morton

Listed as *Mortun* and *Mortune* in the eleventh century, the first element here is identical with Morley. Here the name means the '(place at) the moor or fenland'.

Taking advantage of a blank wall to protest publicly on any subject is by no means confined to the modern era. **The Live & Let Live** is found throughout the country, and is an obvious comment by the owner and/or landlord on a contentious issue of the time, be it the unfair actions of a rival pub, national taxes, or international conflict. Sadly the number of issues which may have been commented on in this way are so numerous that hardly any examples of this pub name can be attributed to a specific circumstance or event.

Mosborough

Although sometimes given as Mosbrough, the origins are still clearly the 'fortified place in moorland'.

Mugginton

Records give the earliest forms as *Mogintun*, *Mugginton* and *Mokyncton*, the modern form first appearing as early as 1242. This Saxon place-name is 'the settlement of the people or followers of Muca' (although the personal name here could have been Mucga).

N

Needham

More accurately High Needham, this place is recorded as *Nedham* in 1244. The first element here is Old English *nied*, meaning 'needy, distress, hardship, poverty', and it is used here as 'the needy or poor homestead'.

Netherseal

Listings such as *Scella* in Domesday and *Scheile* in 1225 show this to be the '(place at) the little copse', from Old English *scegel*. Netherseal has long been the most southerly point in the county. Indeed, until the boundary changes in the 1970s the county (and Netherseal) extended to a single point where it met neighbouring Leicestershire, Staffordshire and Warwickshire. That point is still marked by **The Four Counties** public house. Traditionally the inn had four rooms, one in each county, and it was said that those who had fallen foul of the law in one county could retire to another room and be beyond the reach of jurisdiction.

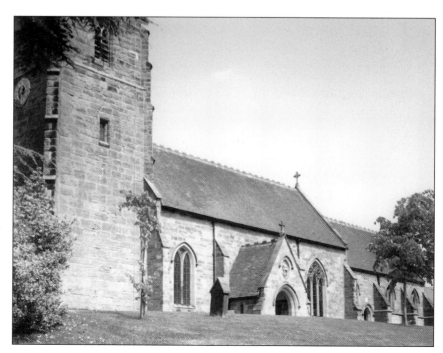

The church at Netherseal.

Newbold

Early records include *Newebold* in Domesday and *Neubaude* in 1226, which show this name to be derived from the Old English for 'the new building'.

Brierley Wood is easily seen to be named from the 'woodland clearing where briars grow', but early recordings of **Brockwell Hill** (and **Lane**) do not confirm whether this was Old English *broc-hyll* or *brocc-hol*, 'the hill by a brook' or 'the badger hole' respectively.

New Mills

An obvious but wrongly plural place-name which refers to a single mill on the right bank of the Goyt, which was there in 1640. Before the construction of the new mill this place was known as Bowden, which is connected with Bowden Hall at Chapel-en-le-Frith and is derived from 'curved, rounded hill', which is not at all applicable here.

Minor place-names of note include **Beard Hall** from the Old English *brerd*, 'brim, margin, hill-side', and **Cown Edge Rocks**, named from 'the ridge above the Colun', which is the former name of the River Sett. From Saxon *cniht-wic*, meaning 'the dairy farm of the young men', comes the modern name of **Knightwake**, and **Joule Bridge** and **Gowhole** are reminders of the Joule family who once lived here. The unusual name **Strines** simply means 'stream, water-course', while **Loe Laughton** was originally the Saxon *low leac-tun*, '(place at) the lower kitchen garden'.

Newton

There are three Newtons in Derbyshire, each having identifying additions as this is one of the most common place-names in the land. Kings Newton is obviously 'the new homestead', which in this case stands on land belonging to the Crown. Newton Solney, another 'new homestead', was held by Alfred de Suleini in 1204. The family name is taken from Subligny near Avranches in France. Newton Grange is 'the new homestead on the hill'. Locally **Hanson Grange**, 'Hynci's hill', and **Moat Low**, 'the assembly hill', tell us about the landscape here without the need to consult the contour lines on the map.

The thatched roof of the **Hardinge Arms** at Kings Newton provided the rather unusual nursery for a single apple-tree seedling in the latter half of the nineteenth century. William Taylor, landlord at the time, was also a keen gardener. Removing the plant, he grew it on in a pot before transferring it to his garden where it flourished. By the 1880s a succession of graftings had increased the number of trees bearing apples and the Newton Wonder, as it was called, was gaining a reputation. Before long a Nottingham company had purchased all but the original tree and the fruit was soon making money in the markets of the world. The original tree lasted until the Second World War when the trunk split in two (and subsequently provided firewood for the locals).

Within the parish of Newton Solney are **Bladon House**, which was built on 'the cold, cheerless hill', and **Wranglands**, which comes from the days when strips of land were rented by local families from the landholder or lords of the manor. The rent was paid either with money they earned from selling produce or more often with a proportion of the crops gathered at harvest time. The name comes from 'crooked strips in the open field'. Why the strips of land were crooked is not recorded.

Noe, River

Listed as *Noue* in 1300, this name is without doubt derived from the Old British or Celtic language. Although we have no idea what the word of origin may be, we can see a connection with other river-names. In Germany the rivers **Naab** and **Nahe** are derived from the root *snau*, meaning 'to flow', also found in Greek *nao* and Latin *natare*, 'to swim'.

Norbury

With eleventh-century records giving *Nordberie* and *Norburi*, this is clearly derived from the Old English for 'the northern fortified place'.

Normanton

There are three Normantons in Derbyshire. The first, near Derby, is simply Normanton and is derived from the Saxon for 'tun (settlement) of the northmen or Norwegians'. The second is South Normanton, which has an addition telling us of 'the tun of the northmen or Norwegians to the south'. The third is Temple Normanton, 'the tun of the northmen or Norwegians under the Knights Templar' (from 1185).

South Normanton is the home of **The Hawthorns** public house. The sign may depict a bush, but the true origins are an heraldic reference to Henry VII. There is strong evidence to suggest this may be one of the earliest inn signs/names, in use since Roman times.

The Romans considered the hawthorn bush to be the definitive protection against sorcery and traditionally placed its leaves in the cradles of their babies. Here, too, is **Carnfield Hall**, which comes from the Old Norse *kerling thveit*, meaning 'old woman's woodland clearing'.

Norton

There are no surprises with the origins, 'the north tun or settlement', but as it is probably the most common of English place-names we would expect to find a second definitive element. Unusually there is no addition here to make it stand out. Minor names here do have additions, including **Norton Green**, **Norton Hall**, **Norton Hammer**, **Norton Lane**, **Norton Lees**, **Norton Park**, **Norton Woodseats** and **Little Norton**. Other names of note include **Maugerhay**, which is 'Malger's enclosure', while 'John's dwelling' was in or near **Chancet Wood**.

O

Oakerthorpe

Recorded in the thirteenth century as *Ulchilthorp* and *Hulkerthorpe*, this is a name of Old Scandinavian origin meaning 'Ulfkell's outlying or secondary farmstead'.

The **Peacock Hotel** here is probably an heraldic reference to the Manners family, Earls and Dukes of Rutland. The town of Oakerthorpe lies in the Amber Valley, which is the origin of the **Amber Hotel**.

Ockbrook

The only early record is Domesday's *Ochebroc*, which tells us of 'Occa's brook'.

The **Royal Oak** is the second most common pub name in the country, so clearly it has an important historical inspiration. Following his defeat by the Parliamentarians at the Battle of Worcester in 1651, Charles II hid from the

The Cross Keys public house at Ockbrook is symbolic of St Peter, although the church is not dedicated to this saint.

Roundheads in the Boscobel Oak near Shifnal, Shropshire. After the restoration of the monarchy it was declared that the returning king's birthday, 29 May, should henceforth be known as Royal Oak Day. Doubtless the Royal Oak public houses throughout the land did a roaring trade on that day.

Offcote

An Old English name recorded as *Ophidescotes* in Domesday, *Offidecot* in 1251 and *Offedecote* in 1265, it originates from 'Offede's cottage(s)'.

Offerton

Early records as *Offretune* and *Offerton* point to 'Offan's tun or settlement', Offan being the only known personal name that fits this place-name.

Ogston

Recorded as *Oggodestun* in 1002, *Oggedestun* in 1004 and *Oughedestune* in 1086, this is a Saxon place-name meaning 'Oggod's tun or settlement'.

Osleton

'Oslaf's tun or settlement' is a Saxon name recorded as both *Olslavestune* and *Oslaueston*.

Osmaston

There are two Osmastons in Derbyshire, one near Derby and the other near Ashbourne. Both have identical early forms as *Osmundestune* and *Osemondestun*, and both originated as 'Osmund's tun or settlement'. There is no reason to believe the places referred to the same person. There are also local names including **Osmaston Coppice** and **Osmaston Pastures**.

Outseats

Even today the name suggests an outlying estate, exactly as it did when it was first coined by the Saxons. From the Old English *ut-seate*, this place-name means 'the outlying settlement', i.e. away from Hathersage.

P

Padfield

It is recorded as *Padefeld* in Domesday and *Paddefeld* a century later, but these are insufficient for us to choose between two alternative definitions of this place-name. The most likely is a personal name, giving 'Pedda's *feld* (cleared land)'. However, Pedda started off as a nickname, and is itself derived from the Old English *pade*, meaning 'toad' or 'amphibian'. Hence the name could also be defined as 'the cleared land frequented by toads or frogs'.

The **Peel Arms Hotel** marks the achievements of the Peel family, particularly its most famous son Sir Robert Peel, who served two terms as prime minister and is best remembered for laying the foundations of the modern police force.

Padley

As with Padfield the first element is either a personal name or the Old English *pade*. Here the second element is *leah*, 'woodland clearing'.

Palterton

Recorded as *Palterton* and *Paltertune*, this name comes from the Old English *pall-torr-tun*, literally 'ledge-hill-settlement'.

Parwich

Recorded as *Peuerwich*, *Pevrewic* and *Peuerwiz*, this is 'the wic on the River Pever'. The Old English *wic* is used in a variety of senses, the most common being a specialised farm, normally referring to a dairy farm. Local names of identical origin include **Parwich Hill**, **Parwich Lees** and **Parwichmoor**. **Gibbonsbank** and **Lombard's Green** recall landowners Henry Gibbon (1670) and Bruno Lambard (thirteenth century) respectively. Nearby Nottinghamshire's most mispronounced place-name, thanks largely to the US television series 'Batman' in the 1960s, is Gotham. Derbyshire, too, has a **Gotham**, which was certainly transferred here by migrants from its counterpart, and thus it probably never was 'the homestead of the goat herders', as was the original.

Peak

The early records of *Pecsoetna*, *Peaclond*, *Pec* and *Pech* all derive from the Saxon *peac*, meaning 'hill, peak'. This word can be compared to the Dutch *pok*, 'dagger', Swedish *polk*, 'cudgel', Swedish dialect *pjuk*, 'point, hillock', and Norwegian *paul*, 'a stick'.

Gautries Hill was the site of 'the trees of the gallows', while another created and rather fanciful name is found at **Clear The Way Mine**.

Peakshole Water

Peak Cavern is one of the most visited of the numerous natural wonders of the Peak District. This huge limestone cavern has been eroded by the underground streams which emerge from the cavern as Peakshole Water. However, neither the river nor the cavern's modern names are quite what was intended when these features were first described and named.

Early records include *aqam de Pekisersse* in 1308, *aqam vocat the Pekisers* in 1455, *Bemrose aqua de Pekeserse* in 1544, *aquam de Peakesarse* in 1636, *Peakes Arse River* in 1654 and *Peakshold River* in 1730. The version from 1654 was still used until the Victorian era when straight-laced tourists regarded the name as somewhat vulgar and maps of the area were 'amended' accordingly. In Anglo-Saxon times of course such words had no unfortunate connotations and were just words. Peakes Arse River simply described the river emerging from the cavern, which it helped to form by eroding the soft rock and dumping the resulting waste soon after returning above ground.

Pentrich

This Old British or Celtic name is recorded as *Pentric*, *Pentrich* and *Pentriz*. This place is derived from two words related to Welsh *pen*, 'hill', and *tyrch*, 'boar', hence it is 'the place at the hill frequented by boars'.

On Main Road stands the **Dog Inn**, a simple sign, and one that is often seen in heraldic circles. The breed depicted on the sign today is often a matter of personal preference and rarely gives any clue as to the heraldic origins, or perhaps the companion of a former innkeeper.

Pilsbury

Domesday's record as *Pilesberie* is sufficient to define this place as 'Pil's fortified place'.

Pilsley

There are two Pilsleys in Derbyshire. The one to the south-east of Chesterfield is recorded as *Pilleslege* in 1002, *Pinneslei* in 1086, *Pileslea* in 1170 and *Pillesleg* in 1226. This is a Saxon place-name meaning 'Pinnel's woodland clearing'.

The other, near Edensor, is found as *Pirelaie* and *Pilisleg*, which show this to have a different personal name, being 'Pil's woodland clearing'.

William Ewart Gladstone (1809–98) dominated the Liberal Party from 1868 to 1894, during which time he and Benjamin Disraeli led Britain to great advances in the industrial boom of the Victorian era. Even a century after his death this four-times prime minister is lauded for his memorable oratory and his instinctive insight into national and international fiscal dealings. His efforts certainly merit the naming of the **Gladstone Arms** in his honour.

Pinxton

This is an unusual name with somewhat unusual origins. The Old British language from pre-Roman times has left its mark on numerous place-names, particularly with regard to topographical features such as hills and rivers, and hence to settlements whose names are derived from them. Recorded as *Penkeston, Penekeston* and *Penkiston*, Pinxton comes from the British *pen-cet* and the Old English *tun*, giving 'hill wood settlement'.

Locally we find **Sleight's Siding** from the Old Norse *sletta*, meaning 'smooth, level', while **Suff Lane**, from the Old English *sogh lanu*, tells of the 'swamp, bog lane'.

Plaistow

This place near Crich is recorded as *Plaustowe* and *Palgestowe*, pointing to the Old English *plegstow*, meaning 'playground'. Just why this place was considered to be a 'playground' (and by whom) is unknown.

Pleasley

Recorded as *Pleseleia* in 1166, this Saxon name tells us of 'Plesa's woodland clearing'. **Outgang Lane** is a rather odd name derived from 'the out-going lane', which suggests it was for one-way traffic. Perhaps there was a second (unknown) track which allowed travellers to enter Pleasley. More likely it is one of the many roads in the land which are known by two different names, depending on the direction the traveller is going – although usually such examples are much longer thoroughfares.

Postern

The only record we have available is *Posterne* from 1300, which shows this to be derived from the Old English *post-aern*, 'the house made of posts, or timber'.

Priestcliffe

Domesday's *Prestecliue* gives us the Old English elements which make up the name, but without other examples it is difficult to be certain of the actual meaning. Literally this is 'the priests' cliff', which could be interpreted as 'the place at the cliff belonging to the priests' or perhaps there was a cave or suchlike here, in which case it may have been 'the priests' retreat or hermitage'.

Quarndon

From Domesday's *Cornun* to *Querendon* at the end of the twelfth century, this name tells us something of daily life in Saxon times, being the '(place at) the hill where millstones are obtained'. Hereabouts we find **Cob Thorne**, a name derived from the '(place at) the pollarded thorn-bush'. There is another example of a name 'borrowed' from afar in **Montpelier** which, as usual, refers to the most distant boundary of the parish.

R

Radbourne

Listed as *Radeburne, Rabburne, Rodburn* and *Redburna* between 1086 and 1171, this name is of Saxon derivation meaning the '(place at) the stream where reeds grow'.

Ravensdale

The early forms of *Rauenesdale* and *Ravenesdale* do not show conclusively if the first element here is a personal name, giving 'Hraefn's dale', or if it is from the Old English *hraefa*, giving 'raven's dale'.

Repton

As 'the ancient capital of Mercia', Repton's earliest record dates from 745 as *Hrypadun*; over the years this has evolved into the much shorter form we see today. This is an Old English name meaning the '(place at) the hill of the Hrype tribe'.

Repton's renowned school was founded by Sir John Port in 1556. His tomb is in Etwall Church and is a splendid memorial to the man.

Local names of note include **Monsom Lane**, derived from 'Mari's island common in predominantly wet land'; **Spur's Bottom**, not a reference to a poor season for a London soccer club but 'sedge, reed bottom of land'; and **Canada**, which is another distant corner name.

The **Blenheim Inn** is named after an important battle in 1704 during the War of the Spanish Succession, marking victory for the British and Austrian troops over those of France and Bavaria.

Repton's lovely church is dedicated to St Wystan and was built in about AD 975, with extensive alterations in the thirteenth–fifteenth centuries. (Photo: Andy Savage)

Riddings

Listed as *Rydynges* in 1296, this name is derived from the Saxon *ryding*, the '(place at) a clearing'.

Ripley

Early records include *Ripelei* in Domesday, *Rippelenga* in 1176 and *Rippelle* in 1240, which show this to originate from Old English *ripel-leah*, the '(place at) the strip-shaped woodland clearing'.

Another example of a name evolved from an ale stake is that of the **Pear Tree Inn**. It is easy to see how 'the clearing with good pasture' became known as **Butterley**. Less obvious is the origin of **Padley Hall**, 'the woodland clearing frequented by toads', while **Waingroves** refers to the 'waggon hole or clearing'. **Nuttals Park** was held by a Mr J.W. Nuttal in 1846, and William Strelley held **Strelley Court** in 1734.

Risley

Another name of Saxon origins, this is from *hris-leah*, the '(place at) the brushwood-covered woodland clearing'. Early records include Domesday's *Riselei* and *Riseleg* from 1236. **Keys Farm** was held by Mr Keys of Hopton in 1670, while **Scroggs Close** comes from 'brushwood enclosure'.

Robey

The only record is as *Raby* in Domesday, which is exactly the Old Swedish *raby*, also seen in the Old Danish *raaby*, meaning the '(place at) the boundary mark'. Today we have no notion of what marked the boundary, although we must assume it was a prominent and obvious feature in the Saxon era.

Rodsley

Listed as *Redlesleie*, *Redeslei*, *Roddeslea* and *Redisleye* between the end of the eleventh and the early thirteenth centuries, this place-name is derived from the Old English *hreod-leah*, the '(place at) the reedy woodland clearing'.

Rosliston

Restlavestune, Rostlavestona, Roustloviston, Rostlaweston and *Roxlaueston* are just five of the many early forms, all of which were recorded during the thirteenth century, although this place was certainly settled well before the arrival of the Normans. Such a wealth of early forms makes the origin clear as 'Hrothlafe's tun or settlement'.

Roston

As mentioned previously, the element *-ing-* in a place-name indicates 'the people or the followers of' and follows a personal name. Early listings show that Roston incorporated this element until at least the thirteenth century in forms such as *Roschinstone, Rocinton* and *Rossynton.* Hence this is 'the settlement of the people or followers of Hrothsige'.

Rother, River

This is an Old British or Celtic river-name, related to the Welsh *rhy*, meaning 'heavy rain', and *dwfr*, 'water, river', used to describe 'the chief river'. Such a simple term to describe a watercourse may appear to be unhelpful as it seems every single one was referred to as 'river, water, brook or stream' and so on. Yet even in the twenty-first century locals rarely refer to the water coursing through their home town as anything other than 'the river'.

Rowland

Listed as *Ralunt* in Domesday and *Raalund* in 1169, this name is derived from the Old Scandinavian *ra-lundr*, the '(place at) roe deer wood'.

Rowsley

As seen from records such as *Reuslege* and *Rolvesle* in the twelfth century, this is a Saxon place-name originating from the '(place at) Hrothwulf's woodland clearing'.

The **Grouse & Claret** on Bakewell Road is a contrived pub name, designed to suggest a refined and upper-class interior to passers-by.

Rowthorn

Derived from the Old English for the '(place at) the rough thorn bush', this is listed as *Rugetorn* and *Ruethorn* around the eleventh century.

Ryknild Street

Though this is undoubtedly an ancient trackway, it was not a Roman road and thus does not have a Roman name. The name was in fact 'borrowed' from Icknield Street/Way, although it is not recorded as such until post-Conquest times. Thus there is no true definition of Ryknild, although it appears in records of Icknield as *Ricnelde stret* and *Rikelinge stret* (both of which are considered erroneous). Icknield itself is popularly thought to be derived from the Iceni tribe, despite the fact that their influence was restricted to only a small part of the route.

S

Sandiacre

Early records of this place-name include *Sendiacra* in 1179, while a century earlier Domesday's version is identical to the modern form. Another Old English place-name, this is derived from *sandig-aecer*, which is as it seems the '(place at) the region of sandy cultivated ground'.

Sapperton

This is one of those rare place-names that give us an insight into the daily lives of the Anglo-Saxons who lived there. Sapperton has a very unusual first element, possibly unique in English place-names. Listed as *Sapertune* in Domesday and *Sapirton* in 1242, this is the Old English *sapera-tun*, 'the settlement of the soap makers'.

Sawley

Recorded as *Salle* in Domesday, *Sallawa* in 1166 and *Sallowe* in 1242, this settlement was located on or near 'sallow tree hill'.

Scarcliff

We hardly need Domesday's *Scardeclif* or the thirteenth-century record of *Scartheclive* to see that this place-name is derived from the '(place at) the cliff face with a scar or gap'.

Locally we find the 'the woodland clearing where rye grows', which has evolved into the unusual modern form **Rylah**. **Roseland Wood** recalls the family of Thomas and William de Roos who held land here in 1373. **Hills Town** is named after the Revd T.C. Hills, vicar of Bolsover and first chairman of Bolsover Urban District Council. **Ling Lane** comes from the Old Norse *lyng*, meaning 'heather', and **Scrater Plantation** is also of Norse derivation, with *skratti-hagi* telling us of 'the goblin enclosure'.

Scropton

Early forms include *Scrotun*, *Scroftun*, *Screptun* and *Scropton*, which would seem to point to nothing other than the Saxon *screop-tun*, giving 'dress settlement', but this does not seem applicable to a place-name. Therefore either the first element has been corrupted to such a degree as to obscure the true origins, or *screop* is correct and the sense is unknown.

Sedsall

Listed as *Segessale* in Domesday and *Seggeshal* in 1275, Sedsall is derived from the Saxon for 'Secg's nook of land'.

Shardlow

Early forms of this eighteenth-century canal port are plentiful and include *Serdelau*, *Serdelaw*, *Sherdelawe* and *Schardelow*, telling us the settlement was situated near a 'mound with a notch or indentation'. Today there are no signs of an artificial mound or tumulus, so we must assume the feature was natural.

Standing near the village pond the **Dog & Duck** recalls duck-hunting in the style much enjoyed by Charles II in particular. Although today's signs invariably portray a man with a gun and a retriever, the original method was very different. The ducks were first caught and their wings pinned before they were released back on to the pond. When the dogs were released the birds' only method of escape was to dive. The sport remained popular until the nineteenth century.

The Navigation public house is named after a word used to describe a canal. Those who built the canals became known as 'navvies', which today is used to describe any labourer doing heavy work.

Shatton

From the Old English *scead-tun*, and recorded as *Scetune* in Domesday and *Scatton* in 1230, this was once 'the settlement on the boundary'.

Sheaf, River

This river-name is derived from the Old English *sceap*, 'boundary', referring to its use as the boundary marker with neighbouring Yorkshire.

Sheldon

This place near Haddon is listed as *Scelhadun* in Domesday and *Schelehaddon* in 1230. The name is derived from the Middle English *schele*, 'shed, hut', and *haddon*, 'belonging to' or 'of' – presumably referring to an outlying or dependent settlement.

There can be no doubt of your location when entering Shipley with its huge town sign.

Shipley

Listed as *Scipelie* in Domesday and *Shippelaea* a century later, the name is derived from the Old English for the '(place at) the pasture for sheep'.

Shirebrook

Listed as *Scirebroc* in 1202, this name describes the '(place at) the bright stream'. In 1421 one Ralph de Stuffin de Wodehous and his family gave their name to **Stuffynwood Hall**.

Shirland

With records as *Sirelunt*, *Sirlund* and *Schirlund* in the eleventh, twelfth and thirteenth centuries respectively, this name is seen as 'the grove of the shire', doubtless the site of an old meeting-place.

The Hay public house is clearly an agricultural reference, while **The Woolpack** is similarly a reminder that the area was (and still is) important for rearing sheep.

Shirley

Despite the early records as *Sirelei* in Domesday, *Schyrelayg* in 1230 and *Schirleg* in 1247, it is impossible to say whether this is derived from the Saxon for the '(place at) the woodland clearing belonging to the shire', or the 'woodland clearing where the shire moot (meeting) is held'.

The Saracens Head is a pub name derived from the arms of a family whose ancestors fought on one of the Crusades in the Holy Land against the Saracens.

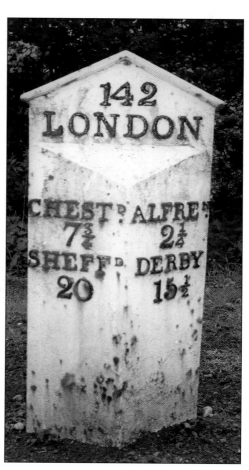

Milepost at Shirland.

The Hay public house, Shirland.

Shottle

Listed as *Sothelle* in Domesday and *Schethell* a century later, this is of Old English origin meaning the '(place at) the hill with a steep slope'.

Siney Sitch

Another of the many interesting minor water names, Siney Sitch flows into Dunge Brook. What appears to be a rather complex name is simply derived from the local dialect verb *sine*, meaning 'to drain'.

Sinfin

Sydenfen, *Sudenfen* and *Sidenfern*, all recorded in the thirteenth century, show this to be a Saxon name meaning the '(place at) the broad fen'.

Smalley

Listed as *Smalleage* in 1009, *Smalei* in Domesday and *Smalleg* in 1226, the second element is Saxon *leah*, 'woodland clearing or glade'. The first element is not 'small' as we might expect, but rather 'narrow'.

Smisby

An Old Scandinavian name recorded as *Sinitretone* in Domesday and *Smidesbi* in 1166, this is 'the smith's village' where smith refers to the trade rather than to a family name.

Snelston

The early records of this place-name all point to this being 'Snell's farm', yet none of them can enable us to say if Snell and his people were Norsemen or Saxons, for the personal name Snell is found in both tongues.

John Roe's Covert was held by John Roe as recently as 1846, while another local name is **Knaveholm**, a much older place-name derived from the '(place at) the servants' marshy meadow'.

Somercotes

This name is Saxon in origin and means exactly what it seems – 'the cottages used in summer'.

The New Inn is a common name, although very few can today be considered 'new'. (Indeed, the Newer Inn would have been more accurate!) However, the presence of a New Inn is interesting as it tells us there was already an inn here when this place was opened. **The Rifle Volunteer** recalls the volunteer soldiers of yesteryear. Such was their commitment to the cause that they paid for their own training before being allowed to become part of the nation's fighting force. What's more, they were also expected to supply their own rifles.

Somersall

This is the name of two Saxon settlements in Derbyshire, each of which acquired a distinctive prefix in the thirteenth century. Listings as *Summersdale* in Domesday and *Sumereshala* a century later show it to be derived from 'Sumor's nook of land'. In 1278 we find a record of *Chirchsomerashal*, today's Church Somersall, while **Somersale Herbert** is reversed today as Herbert Somersall. This character is referred to indirectly in a document dating from 1206 naming the landholder as William, son of Herbert. The close proximity

The Royal Tiger public house at Somercotes.

of the two places would suggest that the personal name Sumor in the place-names refers to the same person.

Spondon

Recorded as *Spondune* in 1086, *Spondon* in 1170 and *Spandon* in 1177, this place-name is the '(place at) the hill where shingles are made' and is derived from the Old English *spon*, 'to chip'.

The Malt Shovel public house is named after an implement used in the brewing process.

Spondon was rebuilt after a fire had destroyed well-nigh the entire village in 1340, after which the residents were given a tax-free year in order to help with the rebuilding of their homes and the church.

Two local names here are worth special attention. The unusual **The Stryne** is basically 'stream', although it is probably more intended to mean 'water channel'. **Megaloughton Lane** is, as far as this author is aware, a unique name in England. Recorded as *Meg' oth' Lanthorn* in 1825, it refers to a phenomenon called a will-o'-the-wisp, which is known as 'Peggy Lantern' in these parts. Properly called *ignis fatuus*, this phosphorescent light seen over swampy ground at night is caused by the spontaneous combustion of methane and other gases emitted by rotting organic matter.

Stainsby

There is only one early record of note here, that as *Steinesbi* in Domesday. The lack of alternative forms means we are unable to see this as anything other than 'Stein's village', from the Old Scandinavian *by* (*see also* Stenson).

Stanley

Two common Saxon elements are found here in *stan-leah*, although it is unusual to find them in combination without further additions. Listed as *Stanlei* in Domesday and *Stanlega* in 1169, this is the '(place at) the stony woodland clearing'.

Stanton

Listed as *Stantune* in 1086, *Staunton* in 1202 and *Stantone* in 1291, this is a fairly common place-name, always originating from 'the farm on stony ground'. Locally we find **Andle Stone**, a corruption of 'anvil' referring to the shape, and **Pilhough**. With the records available it is impossible to say whether this is the 'nook of land where pill-oats are grown' or the 'nook of land where oats whose husks peel off are grown'.

The **Flying Childers Inn** is named after a racehorse which won numerous races in the 1740s, aided by the training of Sir Hugh Childers.

Stapenhill

Early records show this to be from the Old English for the '(place at) the steep hill', while the same records show how *stapol,* meaning 'pillar', has influenced the name's evolution into the modern form.

Here the Battle of Waterloo is marked by **Waterloo Clump**, probably for no reason other than national pride, as there is no reason to believe any local resident took part in that momentous battle.

Staveley

Recorded as *Stavelei* in 1086 and *Staveleia* in 1212, this place-name is derived from the '(place at) the wood where staves are obtained'.

The Nags Head is one of the most common pub names in England, derived from the small riding horse or pony available for hire in the days when horses provided the principal form of transport. Modern sign painters often take advantage of the alternative meaning to depict the name humorously. Before the ladies take offence, perhaps it should be noted that the noun 'nag', meaning

The old watermill at Stainsby has been fully restored and is open to visitors.

someone who complains constantly, is officially applied to those of a masculine gender. **The Beechers Brook** is certainly named after the most famous fence in the Grand National at Aintree. However, the spelling of the pub name is incorrect for the fence was named after Captain Becher, who won the first race in 1839 and subsequently fell at this fence in another year.

The **Hague** has no connection with the Netherlands but is derived from 'the enclosure'. **Holbrook** comes from 'the brook in a hollow', and **Inkersall** from 'Hynkere's hill', itself a nickname meaning 'limping, the lame one'. **Foxlowe Plantation** was held by Samuel Foxlowe in 1765, while **Ince Barn** was held by Richard Ince de Spinkhull in 1496. Francis Marples lived at **Marples Cottages** from at least 1670 and **Mastin Moor** was held by William Masten in 1617. **Parker's Wood** was under the control of John Parker in 1535, and **Morton Lane** is first recorded in 1714, when John Morton was the head of a prominent local family.

Steetley

The fourteenth-century listing as *Stiveleia* shows this to be 'stump leah'. The second element is Old English for a natural woodland clearing, or glade, but the reference to a stump would suggest that a tree had been felled here at some point, which is contradictory to the meaning of *leah*. Normally a fallen tree is uprooted, although it is possible that the stump here was the result of a natural occurrence, perhaps a lightning strike. Whatever the reason, the stump in question would have been notable by virtue of its size or shape.

Stenson

Listed as *Steintune* in Domesday and *Steineston* in 1206, this name has an identical meaning to Stainsby, 'Stein's village'. The difference in the evolution of the two names can be explained in part by Stenson being a Saxon name, while Stainsby has Scandinavian origins.

Sterndale

Listed as *Sternedale* in 1251, *Stenredal* in 1263 and *Stenerdale* in 1288, this place-name is of Saxon origin meaning the '(place at) the stony valley'.

The **Quiet Woman Inn** is a name derived from a very old joke told across Europe. Some signs carry the rhyme: 'Here is a woman who has lost her head. She's quiet now – you see she's dead.'

Stoke

This is the single most common place-name in the country, which explains why so many Stokes here have double-barrelled names. Derived from the Old English *stoc*, it is defined as a 'special place'. Just how 'special' this particular Stoke was is not recorded, but it could have been anything from an outlying farmstead of special significance to a meeting-place, or even a place of worship. Locally we find **Henicar**, an Old Scandinavian name with the suffix formed from *kjarr*, giving 'Hennie's marsh overgrown with brushwood'.

Stretton

From the Old English *straet-tun*, which is exactly how it appears in a record of 1002, this is 'the settlement on the Roman road'.

   Sidney's Farm does not derive from a personal name but from Saxon *sid halh*, the '(place at) the broad corner of land'. **Fletcherhill** was held by William Fletcher in 1603.

Strickle Brook

Flowing near Stainsby and Heath, both of which record the name, this is not as it may seem a corruption of Stockley Brook (into which it empties). Early forms show this to have identical origins to **Sicklebrook Farm**, as 'very small stream'. Hence it is Stockley which is the corrupted version, while Strickle was certainly influenced by the dialect word *strickle*, 'trickles'.

Sturston

Listed as *Sturstone* in Domesday and *Stirstone* in 1226, this Old English name tells us of 'Styr's settlement'.

Sudbury

Several Sudburys are found throughout England, and all of them have identical origins as the Saxon term for 'the southern fortified place'. Another quite common place-name element is found in **Mackley House**, where the first element is the personal name Macca, here suffixed with the Saxon *leah*, 'a woodland clearing'. **St Brides** is reminiscent of the chapel dedicated to that saint which was built in about 1260 and was a place of regular worship until at least 1620.

The church at Stretton is dedicated to St Michael and contains the tombs of many ecclesiastics associated with it.

Sutton

Also known as Sutton on the Hill, this common place-name is simply 'the southern farmstead'. The addition 'on the hill' is not found until the seventeenth century. **Dish Lane** runs through a natural hollow and is recorded as *Dysh lane yate* in 1656, informing us that it was the entrance to an enclosure.

Swadlincote

With records such as *Sivardingescotes* in Domesday, *Suartlincot* in 1208, *Swardlincote* in 1309 and *Swartlyngcote* in 1330, the definition of the name varies depending on whether the personal name in question refers to a Saxon ('Swearthling's cottage'), or a Scandinavian gentleman ('Svartlingr's cottage').

The **Bear Inn** recalls an animal featured in the arms of many noble families. Although heraldic names are normally identified by the addition of a colour, the only alternative here would be a reference to the barbaric sport of bear-baiting which was made illegal in 1835. Such a name is unlikely as it would have been thought to deter potential customers. Remembered as probably the finest designer of steam locomotives this country ever produced, the **Sir Nigel Gresley** in Market Street is a memorial to the man, not the locomotive. Traditionally **The Angel** is a name reminiscent of the connection between religious establishments and taverns. However, the sign at Swadlincote depicts a young, literally angelic, child.

The **Cathems Inn** was known as the Station Hotel until 1969, five years after the station itself had closed. This was also the terminus of the tramway until 1929, so the locals would be able to 'Catch 'em all ways' – i.e. could choose between train and tram.

Swanwick

Recorded as *Swanswyck* in 1278, this name comes from the Old English meaning 'wic of the swine herds', with *wic* as always describing a specialised farm.

The **Steam Packet** remembers a time when parcels, letters and people were carried on such vessels, which may have had some connection with the owner or landlord.

Swarkeston

Home to what is widely thought to be the oldest causeway in England still in use (although a bridge now snakes across the 1,200-metre wide river), Swarkeston is listed as *Suerchestune* in 1086 and *Swerkeston* in 1230, the suffix being Old English *tun*, 'settlement'. Oddly the first element is Scandinavian,

The Railway Inn at Swadlincote.

Above: *Mine cars at Swanwick.*
Left: *Well-dressing at Swanwick.*

although as with Swadlincote the actual personal name involved depends entirely on which language is involved: Old Norse would give 'Suoerkuir's tun', Old Danish 'Swerkir's tun' and Old Swedish 'Swerker's tun'.

Tradition has it that **Scotland Brook** was named by the followers of Bonnie Prince Charlie, who were stopped here on their march to London by the wide river. It is said that the river ran red with the blood of the valiant Scots, but this is mere legend for the true origin of Scotland Brook is the Saxon *scot*, which means 'a narrow stream, a cutting'.

T

Taddington

Recorded as *Tadintune* in Domesday, *Tatinton* in 1200 and *Tatingtone* in 1275, this place-name is Old English in origin. The true Saxon form would have been *Tata-inga-tun*, 'the settlement of the people or followers of Tata'. Although the earliest written record dates from the late eleventh century, people have been living here for millennia, as evidenced by the nearby Five Wells barrow, which, at 1,400 feet above sea-level, is the highest megalithic tomb in England.

Among the unremarkable collection of minor names in Taddington is **Dimin Dale**, which has defied interpretation for many years. Yet there is another Dimin Dale in Devon which may offer an important clue as to the origins. Oddly, it is the very fact that 'Dale' as a place-name is simply not found in Devon which tells us that this must have been transferred from elsewhere, pointing us back to Derbyshire. The only other link between the two places is mining, suggesting that miners may have moved from Derbyshire to Devon, taking their name with them. While this hardly qualifies as a definition, it does point to 'Dimin' being derived from a dialect word used by miners, narrowing the search considerably.

Tansley

Listed as *Teneslege* in Domesday in 1086 and as *Taneslea* in 1175, the etymology of this place-name is somewhat unusual. The second element is the Old English *leah*, 'woodland clearing', while the first element is thought to be the Old English *tan*, meaning 'branch'. If this is correct then the meaning is the '(place at) the woodland clearing in a valley branching off from the main dale'.

Staleyground was held by George Staley by 1846, while at some time precious metal was discovered at **Goldhill** (or perhaps iron pyrites – otherwise known as fool's gold).

Tapton

Early records do not make clear if this is derived from the personal name Tap(p)a or Tap(p)i, although the suffix is undoubtedly Saxon *tun*, 'farmstead'. However, we can be sure that the local **Swaddale Farm** is derived from the 'valley with a path or trackway'; the farm would have been situated either across or alongside the path. George Inman held land around **Inman Well** in 1634, and the area known as **Sidlings** is derived from the Old English *sidling-feld*, meaning 'long heather enclosure'.

Thornhill

As it seems, this is the '(place at or by) the hill overgrown with thorn bushes', and it is recorded as *Thornhull* in 1230. Leading out of the village is **Yorkshire Bridge**, carrying the road to the neighbouring county.

Thornsett

Listed as *Tornesete* in Domesday and *Thorneset* two centuries later, this place-name has the same first element as Thornhill. Here the Old English origin means the '(place at) the fold by the thorn bushes'.

Thorpe

This is listed as *Torp* in Domesday and there can be no doubt that it is 'the outlying farmstead', from the Old English *thorp*. Another record from 1323 lists the place as *Thorpe in the Clottes*, a reference to nearby **Thorpe Cloud**, with the 'cloud' derived from clud, 'hill'.

Local names include **Broadlowash**, the '(place at) the broad burial-mound or hill'; **Spend Lane**, from the Old English *spenn*, 'fence, hedge'; and **Wintercroft Lane**, which led to or ran alongside the 'land used all year round'.

The sign at the Dog & Partridge, Thorpe.

Thulston

Records as *Turuluestun*, *Torulfestune* and *Turleston* help us to identify this place as 'Thurulf's tun or settlement'.

Thurvaston

With listings as *Turverdestune* and *Turwerdeston* in the eleventh and twelfth centuries respectively, this is 'Thurferd's tun or settlement'.

Tibshelf

Records show this name as *Tybbschelfe* in 1179 and *Tibecel* a century earlier in Domesday. Despite the differences between these and other records, there is no doubt that this is the '(place at) Tibba's slope'.

Ticknall

Records from 1002 to 1177 as *Ticenheale*, *Tickenhalle* and *Tikenhala* show the Saxon origin here to be *ticcen-halh*, meaning the '(place at) the nook of land where kids (young goats) are found'. The major natural water source of **Seven Spouts** tells us this was where 'seven springs' rose to the surface.

The **Staff of Life** public house is named to indicate that food is on offer within. The sign depicts a loaf of bread.

The **Chequers Inn** is one of the earliest pub names, dating from the time of the Romans in Britain. The sign, and thus the name, would have informed potential patrons that a game similar to draughts was played within. The sign also doubled as an indicator of a money-lender in later years, and is the basis for the modern word 'exchequer'. We can be confident that this was a Roman name as strong archaeological evidence for the board game is found among the ruins of Pompeii.

Local names include the somewhat unusual **The Scaddows**, which originates from 'boundary enclosure' and refers to its location on the border with the neighbouring parish of Repton.

Above: *The Royal Oak public house at Tibshelf.*
Opposite: *Winkpenny Lane sign at Tibshelf.*

Tideswell

Early records differ little from the modern form and, assuming these are reasonably accurate, this place-name is thus Saxon 'Tidi's stream' or perhaps 'Tidi's place by a stream'. The personal name is also seen locally in **Tideslow**, 'Tidi's burial-mound'. **Weeding Well** speaks of 'the spring near which withies grow'. The local thoroughfare named **Conjoint Lane** is derived from 'Congin's gata', with the Old English *gata* referring to the entrance (and presumably exit) to an enclosure for livestock.

The **Pin Fold** is a common minor place-name, which is comparatively recent in origin. As populations expanded and their livestock proliferated, strays became an increasing source of conflict. By 1787 the problem in Tideswell, particularly with regard to the churchyard of 'the Cathedral of the Peak', had reached the point where something had to be done. So a man was employed to round up the strays and hold them in a special enclosure until they were claimed, on payment of a fine of one shilling. The man so employed was called the pinner and the enclosure the pinfold. This office was filled without a break until 1943 when Mr Joseph Dale, who was also the town crier, died.

Eldon Hole, some 2 miles from Tideswell, although not strictly a 'place', is still a place-name, which may be 'old hill hole', 'fell hill hole' or 'Ella's hill hole'. Several other personal names may also be found here. Unfortunately the early forms are few and too corrupted to offer much assistance. However, the hole itself has a lengthy and well-documented past. One of the earliest records of exploration dates from the latter half of the sixteenth century and involved a peasant who, on the orders of the Earl of Leicester, was lowered down the natural shaft to a depth of 'two hundred ells' (250 metres) and still did not find the bottom. The poor man was so terrified by the experience that he went completely mad and died eight days afterwards. The following century saw another attempt to reach the bottom of Eldon Hole, this time by poet Charles Cotton, who, armed with a lead weight and rope, related his findings in verse:

> But I myself, with half the Peake surrounded,
> Eight hundred, fourscore yards have sounded;
> And though of these fourscore returned back wet,
> The plummet drew and found no bottom yet;
> Though when I went to make a new essay,
> I could not get the lead down half the way.

The next attempt of note was led by Mr John Lloyd in 1770. He was lowered 'exactly 62 yards down', and found himself in a small recess giving access to a domed cavern estimated at 50 metres in diameter. He noted, but did not explore, a series of other caverns and recesses, and then returned to the surface. There he was told by a local man that a second shaft in the floor of the cavern, which 'went down a great depth', had recently been covered by lead miners. This second shaft perhaps explains the conflicting measurements achieved by Charles Cotton.

Around the time of Mr Lloyd's descent, and again at the end of the eighteenth century, miners investigated Eldon Hole, not as explorers but detectives. Riderless horses had been found near the entrance and their owners were missing. Assuming they had been robbed and thrown down the abyss, the men set out to search for bodies. Yet not one victim was discovered.

Tissington

Domesday's *Tizinctun*, *Tiscintona* in 1141 and *Ticintona* and *Tysincton* in 1242 all point to the origins of this name as 'the settlement of the people or followers of Tidsige'.

An abundance of local names include **Sharplow**, from the 'sharp, pointed burial-mound'; **Bassett Wood**, which was held by William Basset in 1498, and **Crake Low**, the 'burial-mound where crows or ravens are seen'.

Totley

The element *-inga-* in the Domesday form as *Totingelei* had disappeared by the early thirteenth century when it is listed as *Totenleg*. This place-name is derived from the Old English, telling of the '(place at) the woodland clearing of the people or followers of Tota'.

Well-dressing at Tissington. The scene is of the discovery of the infant Moses.

Trent, River

An Old British river-name, the first element here corresponds with Celtic *tri*, 'across', while the second is akin to the Old Irish *set*, 'journey'. The name is usually defined as 'trespasser', suggesting it floods readily.

Trusley

A record from 1166 gives this place-name as *Trusselai*, which can only describe the '(place at) the woodland clearing with fallen leaves and rubbish'. The purpose of any place-name was to give a brief description of the location, to assist travellers in the days when signposts were unheard of. With this definition of Trusley the normal distinctiveness of any place-name is lost, for there is not a forest, wood, hedgerow or garden on the planet which, if left untended for any length of time, does not readily accumulate leaf litter. Certainly it is difficult to understand the true meaning here.

Tunstead

Listed as *Tounstede* in 1200, this name is derived from the Old English *tun-stede*, 'the settlement with an enclosed pasture' – a rather lengthy description of a farmstead.

Tupton

Listed in Domesday as *Topeslage*, this Saxon name means 'the farm of the rams'. Here we also find **Ankerbold**, which tells us this was once 'the hermit's dwelling'.

Turnditch

This is listed as *Turnyndedyche* in 1346 and *Thornedishe* in 1482, but these and similar records do not clarify whether this is the '(place at) the winding ditch' or the '(place at) the thorny ditch'. What is clear is that John Booler, who was here in 1846, gave his name to **Booler's Wood**.

Twyford

Recorded as *Tuiforde* in 1086 and *Tuiford* in 1206, this is the '(place at) the double ford'. The meaning here could either be where two arms of the same or different rivers are crossed, or two crossing-points close to each other on the same river.

U

Underwood

Listed as *Hunderwude* and *Underwode* in the late thirteenth century, this is an Old English name meaning 'the place within the wood' – literally 'under' the canopy. **Corkley** is a local name which is either 'Corta's clearing' or, if the first element is Old English *cort*, 'the short woodland clearing'. **Ireton Farm** was once 'the farm of the Irishman (or -men)'. **Mugginton** has few early records, which makes it difficult to decide if this is 'Mogga's or Mugga's farmstead'.

Unstone

Recorded as *Onestune*, *Oneston*, *Onistone* and *Honeston* in the thirteenth century, this place-name comes from the Saxon or Old English for 'On's tun or settlement'.

Local minor place-names include **Hallowes Farm**, which is not from a personal name but is derived from the '(place at) the nooks of land', while **Hundall** is easy to recognise as 'the dogs (hounds) hill'.

Wadshelf

Wadshelf near Brampton is listed as *Wadescel* and *Wadescelf* in Domesday. Of Old English derivation, this is 'Wada's hill'.

Walton on Trent

This is a common Old English place-name found in virtually every English county. Listed in Domesday as *Waletune*, it was once 'the farmstead of the Welshmen (or possibly serfs)'.

Around Walton are many minor names including **Hunger Hill**, which is derived from the Old English *hungor*, literally 'hunger, famine', used here to indicate barren, unproductive ground. **Matherbank Plantation** was held by Ralph Mather by 1670. The somewhat simplistic-sounding **Moor Lawn** is listed as *atte-more* in 1394 and is derived from the Old English *mor*, 'barren wasteland', and the Old French or Middle English *launde*, 'open space in woodland'. **Gladwin Wood** was held by one Disimus Gladwin in 1734.

Wardlow

Thirteenth-century listings as *Wardelawe* and *Wardlowe* point to this place-name's origin being 'watch hill', referring to a look-out point.

Wensley

Wensley is recorded as *Wodnesleie* in Domesday and *Wednesleg* in 1212. Wednesday is derived from 'Woden's day' and the two early listings given here show the similarities between the origin and the modern form of the place-name and the day of the week. Wensley is thus of Saxon origin meaning 'the woodland clearing dedicated to Woden' – probably a place of ritual or worship.

Locally we find **Snitterton**, which was 'Syntra's farmstead' by the time the Norman conquest of England had begun. **Cowley Hall** was built on the woodland clearing 'where charcoal is burnt'.

The picturesque town sign at Walton on Trent.

Wessington

This Old English place-name is derived from 'Wigstan's tun or settlement' and is recorded as *Wistanestune* in Domesday and *Wystantowe* in 1252.

Locally we find the minor names **Carr Barn**, derived from the Old Norse *kjarr*, meaning 'brushwood'; **Ouzle Croft**, which continues to show the original Old English *ouzle*, the early name for the blackbird; and **Driftway**, from the later Middle English *drift*, 'cattle road', the additional 'way' is comparatively recent.

Weston

There are two Westons in Derbyshire, sharing a common place-name found all over England and referring to 'the western farmstead'. Weston-upon-Trent's suffix is discussed under the river-name, while Weston Underwood needs no explanation.

Place-names can be divided into several basic groups as far as origins are concerned, and the minor place-names for the Westons have examples from all of them. **Sugar Loaf** is a reference to the shape of the field; **Taghole Lane** ran alongside 'the hollow for young sheep'; **Chilla Car** is a Norse name for 'the cold marshland overgrown with brushwood'; **The Clives** can almost still be seen as 'the cliffs'; **The Clouds** (from clud) refer to 'the rocks'; **Herbalshaw Meadow** tells us this was 'a shelter in the meadow under the ridge'; and **Sarson's Bridge** was held by John Sarson.

Whaley

The only early form known is as *Walley* in 1230, the modern version appearing as early as 1540. The first element here is certainly an old (unknown) word for 'hill', followed by the Saxon *leah*, 'clearing'.

Whatstandwell

This is a place-name that can only belong in England! The only early form of the name is *Watstanwell* in 1510. However, it is well documented that a bridge built over a century earlier in 1390 was named after a Walter Stonewell, near whose house it was erected. It seems likely that this gentleman played a very important role in the construction of the bridge. The names of the **Homesford Cottage Inn** and **Homesford** itself are taken from places at Wheston.

Wheston

Listed as *Whestan* in 1231 and *Whetston* in 1271, this Saxon name recalls 'the whetstone'. Here we find the name of **Cherryslack**, a name which surely could not be found elsewhere in the world, which tells us this was 'the part of the forest fenced off for hunting'. Homesford is a corruption of an uncertain personal name, something akin to 'Hunbeorht's field (cleared land)'.

Whitfield

'The white feld (woodland clearing)' is recorded as *Witfield* in Domesday and *Whitefeld* in 1226. Clearly the region was not actually white in colour, but would have appeared particularly light to the observer.

Whittington

Listed as *Witintune* in Domesday, *Whitinton* in 1194 and *Hwytinton* in 1231, this name of Saxon origin speaks of 'the settlement of the people or followers of

Hwita'. Another of the 'distant' names is found here with **Ballarat Cottages**, which stand at the boundary of the parish.

Hwita's people doubtless kept sheep, and probably named **Sheepcot Liggit** from *sceap*, 'sheep', *cot*, 'cottage', and *hlid-geat*, 'swing-gate'. A millennium or so later several important figures descended on Whittington, specifically on what was to become **Revolution House**. A tablet attached to the cottage tells the story: 'In a room which formerly existed at the end of this cottage [the remaining portions of what was the old **Cock & Pynot**] the Earl of Danby, Earl of Devonshire and Mr John D'Arcy [eldest son of the Earl of Holderness] met some time in 1688 to concert measures which resulted in the Revolution of that year.' Certainly it was not the first such meeting but was one of many which finally led to the Glorious Revolution when William of Orange took the throne. The old inn name features the word 'pynot', an old term for a magpie.

Whitwell

Found in records as early as the mid-tenth century, this is 'the white spring or stream'. 'White' here is used in the sense of 'clear or untainted water'. Some would have us believe that the local name Belph, listed as *Belgh* in 1179, *Bellgh* and *Belgph* in 1590 and *Belphe* in 1591, refers to the same stream that gave its name to Whitwell, specifically to a stretch which could be described as a 'roaring river', from the Old English *Belge*. However, most agree the true origin is *belg*, meaning 'bag', referring to the shape of the valley.

Bakestone Moor, from the Saxon *baec-stan-mor*, tells us this was 'the ridge of stony wasteland', as uncomplimentary a name as **Dumb Hall**, while **Bondhay** was 'the enclosure of the peasant farmer'.

Wigley

All the early records we have are from the thirteenth century, listing the place as *Wiggelay*, *Wikeley*, *Wiggelee* and *Wyggeleg*, telling us this place was at one time 'Wicga's place at the woodland clearing'.

Wigwell

The same personal name is found here as is seen in Wigley, although there is no reason to suppose it refers to the same person. 'Wicga's spring' is found in records as *Wyggewelle*, *Wiggewell* and *Wiggeswalle*.

Willersley

Early thirteenth-century records of *Wildereslay* and *Willardesley* point to the Old English origins as 'Wilheard's woodland clearing'.

Willington

From the Saxon *wilign-tun*, this is 'the willow-tree farm', as seen by records as *Willetune* in 1086, *Wilenton* in 1114, *Wyllingtone* in 1198, *Wyliton* in 1201, *Wylghton* in 1325, *Welynton* in 1390 and *Wellington* in 1577.

Wilne

Two places with this name, differentiated by the additions Great and Church, lie on opposite sides of the River Derwent. There is an island here which must once have been called *Wilne*, derived from the Old English *wilgen-eg*, 'the island of willows'.

Wilsthorpe

There are just two early records, as *Wiuelestorp* in 1169 and *Wivelesthorp* in 1242, showing us that this place-name is derived from Old Scandinavian. However, the personal name is uncertain, giving either 'Wifel's or Vifil's thorp (outlying farmstead)'.

Windley

From the Old English *winn-leah*, and recorded as *Winleg* and *Wynleye* in the latter half of the thirteenth century, this place-name tells of the '(place at or near) the meadow or pasture glade'.

The local name **Champion** is from the Old French *champaigne*, meaning 'open country', and refers to one of the parks of Duffield Frith. **Farnah Hall** sounds as though it was imported from abroad, but is in fact a home-grown name (if Old Norse and Saxon can be considered national tongues) meaning 'fern spring'.

Wingerworth

With early records giving this place as *Wingreurde* and *Wingerwurth*, this can only be 'Winegar's farmstead'. The second element is derived from the Old Scandinavian *thorp*.

Every village blacksmith required a reliable water source and one such is marked by the name of the **Smithy Pond Pub** in Nethermoor Road. The name of **Swathwick** has been recorded in so many differing forms that they do little more than cloud the issue, although the first element is definitely the Saxon *swaedh*, meaning 'a measure of ground' (not a specific measurement such as an acre). There is little doubt the intended sense here can be simplified to the

The sign of the Green Dragon public house at Willington.

'clearing beside a path'. Nearby **Emmet Field Wood** takes its name from the Old English or Saxon *ea-mot*, which is the 'riverside meeting place', in particular where judicial matters were discussed. Lastly the name of **Belfit Hall** recalls former landowner Robert Belfit, who is recorded as being here by 1699.

Wingfield

This is actually two places, North and South Wingfield, the additions being obvious. The name is derived from the Old English for 'grazing ground'.

The **Alma Inn** is quite a common pub name which derives from the battle of 1854 which saw the Allies' first victory over the Russians in the Crimean War. The battle was fought near the River Alma. Early landlords liked to have an instantly recognisable and easily produced sign, such as the **Spinning Wheel Inn**. Minor names in the Wingfields include **Williamthorpe**, 'Willelm's outlying farm'; **Bacon Close**, held by William Bacon in 1829; and **Kiddies Croft**, a somewhat corrupted modern version of what was once the track which led to 'the place where young goats were reared'.

The lost **Limbery Chapel** once stood on 'lime hill', while **Castle Hill** is traditionally held to have been the site of a Roman camp, although archaeological evidence has yet to verify this. **Coalburn Hill** is the hill near the river from which it took its name, 'the cool stream'. **Pearsons Wood** was held by George Pierson in 1639, while **Shrewsbury Cottage** marks lands held by the Earls of Shrewsbury from the fifteenth to the seventeenth century.

Winsley

Listed as *Wiuesleia* in 1097 and *Wynesleye* in 1269, this Saxon place-name is 'Wine's woodland clearing'.

Winster

Records such as *Winsterne* and *Winesterna* show that Winster and Winsley feature the same personal name, although it seems unlikely they refer to the same person. This place-name is derived from the Old English 'Wine's thorn bush'.

The **Old Bowling Green** told customers that the game was played here, while the additional 'Old' informs us that it pre-dated a nearby rival pub. **Trulle Bridge** comes from the Saxon word *thyrel*, meaning 'pierced', thought to be a reference to some accident on or near the bridge, while **White's Wood** was held by George White by 1734.

Wirksworth

The Saxon *worth* refers to a 'fortified enclosure'. Recorded as *Wurcesuuyrthe* in 825, *Werchesuuorde* in Domesday and *Werkewurdo* in 1182, this is 'Weorc's fortified enclosure'.

The well-known phrase used to describe the painstakingly slow progress of officialdom may well owe something to Wirksworth, for the 'red tape' traditionally used to tie up such documents was produced here in the eighteenth and nineteenth centuries.

A similar Saxon personal name occurs in the origin of **Wigwell Grange**, from 'Wicga's spring or stream'. Francis Baylye held **Baileycroft Quarry** in 1610, while **Boulderflats Mine** remembers the fifteenth-century landlord Richard Bulder. **Broxendale Farm** seems to be a typical name referring to 'the brook in the valley', yet the valley is dry and the true origin is 'badger stone valley'.

Woodthorpe

This is derived from the Old Scandinavian *thorp*, 'the fortified enclosure', here 'in a wood'. This place near Staveley is listed in the thirteenth century as *Wodesthorp* and *Wodethorpe*.

Wormhill

Early listings of Wormhill, the birthplace of the canal builder James Brindley in 1716, include *Wruenele*, *Wurmhill*, *Wrmenhulle* and *Wurmehill*, but they do not clarify whether the origin here is 'hill frequented by reptiles' or 'Wyrma's hill'. However, the English climate being what it is, the latter seems more likely.

Locally we find **Hargatewall** derived from 'herd farm near a spring'. **Tomthorn** is recorded in a document dating from the eighteenth century, a document which also has a drawing depicting the thorn-bush which gave the place its name.

Wyaston

Listed as *Widerdestune* in Domesday and *Wyardestone* in 1244, this Old English name is derived from 'Wigheard's tun or settlement'.

Wye, River

This rather unusual river-name dates from pre-Roman times and is derived from the Celtic meaning 'river course'. Unusually, this seems to apply more to the river channel than to the water flow, as we would normally expect.

Y

Yeaveley

In Domesday we find *Gheveli* while two centuries later we have a record of *Yeueleye*, which together enable us to define this Saxon place-name as 'Geofa's woodland clearing'. The unusually named **Stydd Hall** comes from 'the religious house', which in turn refers to premises of the Knights Hospitaller. From the Old English *edisc*, meaning 'the enclosed park', comes the modern name **Eddishes**.

Yeldersley

A place-name of similar origins to Yeaveley, it is recorded as *Geldeslei* in Domesday, and *Yldreslee*, *Yhildrisleye*, *Gildreleg* and *Yhildirleg* during the early thirteenth century. This Saxon name is derived from 'Geldhere's woodland clearing'.

Youlgreave

Listed in Domesday as *Giolgrave*, in 1208 as *Hyolegrave*, in 1259 as *Yolegrave* and in 1285 as *Yolgreue*, this Old English name can easily be seen to be the '(place at) the yellow grove'.